Christian
Psychology

Christian Psychology

TOWARD A NEW SYNTHESIS

John M. McDonagh

Crossroad · New York

ACKNOWLEDGMENTS

Raymond Moody, *Life After Life,* Mockingbird Books Inc.
Used with permission.

1982
The Crossroad Publishing Company
575 Lexington Avenue, New York, NY 10022

Printed in the United States of America

Library of Congress Cataloging in Publication Data

McDonagh, John M.
Christian psychology.

Bibliography: p.
1. Christianity—Psychology. 2. Psychotherapy.
I. Title.

BR110.M38	150.19	81–19454
ISBN 0–8245–0449–6		AACR2

Contents

Introduction

In the personal crisis of my life, how far can psychotherapy
take me? How far do I wish to be taken? Is there a line that
separates the spiritual path from therapeutic progress?
What actually takes place in psychotherapy when seen
against the vision of human nature offered by sacred tradition?

Spiritual guides and psychotherapists, what do your names
mean? How should we accept what you call yourselves?
Behind these names, which of you are the real spiritual
guides and which the real psychotherapists? We need to
know. I need to know.

–Jacob Needleman[1]

In my view, Needleman has posed one of the most searching
and relevant sets of questions that can be asked of modern
psychotherapy. This book represents an attempt to address
some of these questions. It is a book about the relationship
between modern psychology and religion in general, and
modern psychotherapy and the Christian religion in particular. As such, it does not pretend to be a work of "science,"
although a good deal of the material presented is based on the
findings of the social sciences, as well as on the opinions of
many who have earned their reputations as scientists in their
fields. Particularly in the realm of psychotherapy, where the
methods of traditional science are often not adequate, the
writing may sound more like rhetoric. This is no coincidence.
Szasz has made the very astute observation that modern psychotherapy more closely resembles the discipline of "rhetoric" than that of "science" (in the traditional Aristotelian

1

distinction of those terms).[2] It seems appropriate, therefore, that much of what is treated in this work will resemble rhetoric rather than science, as I happen to agree with Szasz on this point.

It is my view that this will enhance rather than diminish the validity of what is presented. It seems to me that it is preferable to state when one is presenting evidence that is, to whatever degree, persuasive, rather than pretend that it is scientific knowledge that purports to be conclusive.

If a book on psychology is not "scientific," there are many who will ask, "What good is it?" I hope to demonstrate that this very question misses a crucial point: namely, that psychology has grown beyond the traditional limits of what is commonly regarded as "science" in Western thought. "Science" has become a straitjacket in the light of recent findings in psychology; yet it is a magic word in our society, and has a kind of hypnotic effect on us. "Science" has unfortunately been equated with "truth" in the minds of many educated people.

Another reason why this book does not adhere to the rubric of science, narrowly defined, is that "scientific" in the area of the social sciences often requires the writer to limit the focus of his or her investigation to the very limited phenomena that lend themselves easily to scientific control, replication, etc. The end result of this process too often winds up dealing with trivia, or with propositions we somehow knew were true before they were investigated "scientifically."

At times, it is an iconoclastic book. It attempts to debunk a great deal of what I regard as unproductive myth in psychology generally, and in psychotherapy in particular. As such, it is written from a point of view. But it is a point of view not without evidence. It is my hope that the presentation of the evidence will be judged to be fair and honest. After all, that is what one expects from a work of rhetoric. In addition, this book is intended to be, above all, *credible* and *meaningful.* It is intended to stimulate dialogue, and not to make final pronouncements. The intent, however, is to *challenge* those who may disagree with the hypotheses presented. The need for more meaningful dialogue between psychology and religion is clear.

The fact that psychotherapy must go beyond the limitations of social science if it is to be more helpful to people is made evident by another quote from Needleman (1976). In discussing the lack of a sense of meaning to life, death, and one's relation to the universe experienced by modern people, he says:

> No one suffers from this lack more than the psychiatrists themselves, more and more of whom despair over their inability to help another human being in the fundamental way they once dreamed possible. . . . They have come to see themselves in the same situation as their patients and the rest of us.[3]

Clearly something is lacking in the social sciences that prevents them from feeding psychotherapy the insights about human nature that it needs in order to be more effective. And the answer does not lie in resorting to the biological sciences to solve these problems. This is not to deny that advances in psychopharmacology have had a great beneficial impact. Such advances have greatly improved the treatment of emotional problems. However, the hunger for psychological well-being persists despite the use of a large variety of therapies. I believe that one reason for this is that contemporary social science has yielded us a very truncated view of the human person. In its attempt to free itself from the dogmatism of religion, it has denigrated religious insights about the nature of human beings, thereby impoverishing itself and shortchanging those it wishes to serve. Modern Western psychotherapy, in its inception and to the present day, did not merely disassociate itself from religion in order to assume a more "enlightened" status as a "science," but has been actively antagonistic to religion. Contemporary psychotherapists who are aware of the limitations of their own craft have been borrowing rather freely from Oriental religions certain metaphysical concepts (e.g., reincarnation and astral projection) and practices (particularly Eastern forms of meditation), and this is perhaps what Needleman was describing when he said, "The shrinks are beginning to sound like gurus." For some reason, Western psychotherapists have not sought out comparable metaphysical concepts and insights that lay right under their noses: namely, those contained in a religion known as Christianity.

The relationship between psychotherapy and organized Christianity got off to a bad start. There is little point in trying to allocate blame for this poor relationship, as it was probably inevitable, owing to the historical circumstances of the birth of modern psychotherapy. Modern psychotherapy (and I am referring here chiefly to psychoanalysis) was a child of the Enlightenment. We know too well the acrimonious relationship between the proponents of the Enlightenment and established or organized Christianity, so that in all likelihood, even if psychoanalysis had made a concerted effort to make peace with the Church, it would still have been viewed with some suspicion. However, it is interesting to note that even in the early days of psychoanalysis, we find Freud making admiring references to Oriental Yoga,[4] and in the same work *(Civilization and its Discontents,* 1930) questioning whether Jesus Christ was a real historical figure or merely a myth (Freud, 1961).[5]

At first glance, it appears curious that modern psychotherapy would exhibit such a congenial and open attitude toward Oriental religions and philosophies while, at the same time, shunning, or even disparaging, Christianity. However, this situation is not at all strange when one considers that the intellectual tradition of which modern psychotherapy is a product had to fight organized Christianity tooth and nail for the right of freedom of inquiry. If we add to that the very important fact that Freud and most of his early disciples were Jewish, we must consider how difficult it must have been for them to view a religion that had been associated with the persecution of their own people with the same cool detachment with which they could view some remote Oriental cult.

One modern thinker has observed that Christianity might qualify as a truly great religion if it were ever put into practice. It is the great scandal of Christianity (quite correctly noted by

Freud in *Civilization and its Discontents*)[6] that it has been associated, whether officially or unofficially, with the shedding of the blood of those who did not accept it, as well as of those Christians who did not accept the predominant local version of the Christian message. In short, it is we Christians who have been chiefly responsible for the difficulty our Jewish brethren often have in viewing positively the teachings of one of their own teachers. Having made that statement, I hope that what follows can be read with more equanimity, by believer and nonbeliever alike.

Still, however, the subject of the relationship between the Christian religion and modern psychology is very difficult to deal with in a detached manner by anyone who has been closely associated with both. A few words on my own background, on where I have been and where I am now, are essential to render this work more credible. My education has, for the most part, been in Catholic schools, with the exception of one year at the University of Strasbourg (my junior year of college) and the years spent at the University of Oklahoma for my doctorate. My personal crisis of faith, however, occurred before either of these exposures to the non-Catholic intellectual world; it was while I was still a sophomore at Fordham College. It was at Fordham that I began to have deep doubts about my Catholic faith, which up to that time had given me chiefly pat answers to problems, which I accepted. In looking back, however, it is with deep gratitude that I realize that my education at Fordham also provided me with the tools to question and arrive at my own answers.

For a considerable period following this "crisis" I settled into a post-Christian type of agnosticism, occasionally interrupted by periods of trying to hang onto some kind of vaguely theistic hope, reinforced by reading such writers as Paul Tillich. Returning from Strasbourg in 1964, I was determined to become a psychologist. While finishing up my degree at Fordham, I attended a course offered by Rollo May at the New School, and also began my own personal therapy. These discoveries of a new way to look at the world and myself were exhilarating.

In the mid-sixties, I saw psychology as the new science that would liberate me from the superstitions of the past, and open up a whole new world in which I would be freer than ever before. Science and reason, rather than traditional religion, I thought, would help liberate others too. Happiness was having a good therapist, and eventually, being one. After fifteen years in the field as a student, teacher, patient, and therapist, disillusionment had begun to replace the youthful missionary fervor. Even teaching, which offered the rare opportunity to influence others, began to lose its appeal when I was obliged to present so many studies of doubtful value. I laughed with a feeling of recognition when I read W. H. Auden's words, "Thou shalt not commit social science." Some would refer to this phenomenon as "burnout," and perhaps it was.

Gradually it was dawning on me that psychotherapy could be regarded in many respects more properly as a religion rather than a science or an art. The incurable empiricist in me began to despair, and entered another crisis of faith. The way of life preached by the therapeutic community was not based on science after all, but on dogma. Of course, I am not denying the very real and invaluable contributions made by psychological research. What has been most disillusioning, however, is the gap between this research and its application, and the subtle injection of personal values into both the research and the therapy that is presumed to be its application. To my mind, these values seem arbitrary, and not, except in some cases, compelled by scientific research. The values of the researchers and the therapists seem to play too important a role in the whole enterprise. I believe that these values should be made more explicit by those involved, and further, that the failure to do so falls regrettably short of intellectual honesty. There is a dominant orthodoxy of values among most in the social sciences (and here I include psychiatry), which the true believers simply refuse to question. This will be examined in the first two chapters of this book.

Let us return briefly to the question of the relative roles that psychotherapy and religion are presumed to play in one's life. Recall Needleman's quote at the beginning of this Introduction, "Is there a line that separates the spiritual path from therapeutic progress?" The existential psychologies realized that what patients often sought from psychotherapy was some ultimate meaning for their lives. Indeed, one of the most popular books dealing with these issues is Viktor Frankl's *Man's Search for Meaning* (1962).[7] The human will to meaning was regarded as central to psychological functioning. Traditionally religion has provided people with answers concerning meaning in the world, but in a religious vacuum it was not surprising that many would seek meaning from their therapy. Having lived in a religious vacuum myself, and dealing every day with patients who lack meaning in their lives, has made this issue very important to me. The existentialist quest for this meaning is the central theme of the third chapter of this book. I would like to mention in passing that Freud himself perceived the role of religion in regard to meaning:

> Once again, only religion can answer the question of the purpose of life. One can hardly be wrong in concluding that the idea of life having a purpose stands and falls with the religious system (1961).[8]

However, Freud says a paragraph later that for the individual "what decides the purpose of life is simply the program of the pleasure principle." Jung and the existentialists, of course, abandoned this view, but it is still the predominant one in psychodynamic and behaviorist psychologies. While I could not agree totally with the theory of the pleasure principle as a source of meaning, I really had nothing better to offer.

Then, by a fortuitous circumstance, I came across a couple of books that began the very complex process of changing my whole gestalt of the relationship between science and religion, which seemed to be particularly relevant to psychology. The books were Raymond Moody's *Life After Life* (1975),[9] and *Reflections on "Life After Life"*(1977).[10] Closely following this was a presentation by psychologist Allen Bergin in New York entitled "Psychotherapy and Religious Values" (1979),[11] which reaffirmed some of the feelings already expressed concerning the inevitable interplay of the therapist's values with his or her therapy. Moody's work gave me the courage to introduce into psychotherapy certain of his findings relating to the near-death experiences of people who had attempted suicide. Moody's book relates that the experiences of would-be suicides were not as pleasant as those who encountered death by illness or accident. In a decidedly unorthodox move, I introduced several suicidal patients to Moody's findings, which challenged them to reassess the possible consequences of suicide. I was gratified to see that it resulted in a sharp drop in suicidal ideation (McDonagh, 1979).[12] Research on near-death experiences still going on (Ring, 1980),[13] and the findings presented by Moody in regard to suicide are not uniformly observed. However, I began to read a great deal about near-death experiences because of what I thought it might have to say about the nature of the human person. Western psychology has assumed that the human personality disintegrates at death and ceases to function. Near-death research has given us serious reason to question this assumption. This research and how it relates to religious conceptions of humanity will serve as the basis of the fourth chapter.

In some respects, this work represents a personal journey, or is the product of a personal journey still underway. I could never have undertaken this work if I had not myself become very selfish, and then seen the folly of it. For many years I managed to avoid seeing how my own selfishness adversely affected other people. And certainly I don't claim to have become sufficiently unselfish now. The struggle against selfishness is never-ending, and that is the beauty and the challenge of Jesus. The term "Christian," I suggest, is, not adequately grasped until it is understood that in this mortal world there are extremely few "accomplished" Christians. To be "accomplished" implies that one is complete. I hope to show in Chapter 5 that the human soul cannot be assumed to be complete in this life. That is the message behind the seemingly unattainable ideals set forth by Jesus. A French priest wrote a little book that sums up this attitude beautifully in its title, *I Shall Never Love Enough* (Huvelin, 1963).[14] My personal journey has included many attempts of moderate success to improve

and "actualize" myself, including different forms of psychotherapy as well as Transcendental Meditation. But the greatest change, without doubt the greatest turning point on this
path, was effected from the time I received the Baptism in the
Holy Spirit, and the inner healing that followed. Hence, it is
with the deepest conviction that I can now state that "it is in
dying that we are born to eternal life," for it is in dying to the
self that we can be awakened from our sleep and made more
alive. But the journey continues, for like Abbé Huvelin, I don't
believe that any of us will ever love enough. That is the chief
way in which the Christian path can be seen in opposition to
the exaltation of the self.

While many (including myself) have, to various degrees,
sought "enlightenment" in Oriental religions, it is my present
conviction that Christianity contains a type of enlightenment
that surpasses that of the Orient. A number of years ago Alan
Watts (1961) wrote:

> Membership in Christ could mean liberation from *maya*
> (illusion) and its categories. . . . In practice it means accepting
> the religion or bondage of the Christian subgroup.[15]

I believe deeply that the insights of Jesus have the power to
liberate us from illusion, but there are many obstacles blocking
that liberation. As for the second part of Watts's quote, the
various strictures of the "Christian subgroup" can be viewed
as "bondage," but most of them are actually means by which
liberation is achieved. Speaking of them globally as "bondage"
makes no sense if one believes in liberation. If there is no
liberation at the end of the path, then the long list Christians
have of "shoulds" and "should nots" does seem oppressive.
Most religions have such lists or disciplines. They are best
viewed as part of freeing the self by denying the self ("self" as
in "selfish"). Of course, if there is no freeing of the self at the
end, why shouldn't these disciplines be seen as oppressive?
Sitting under a tree for several years probably wasn't much
fun for the Buddha. And Jesus probably didn't enjoy fasting in
the desert for forty days either. But what Jesus brought out of
the desert was vastly different from the Buddha's teaching.

Jesus brought a promise of eternal life. He also brought the power to heal, and a philosophy of healing by forgiveness: forgiveness of us by the Father, and forgiveness of each other. By teaching forgiveness, Jesus was also saying that there is such a thing as evil, and that this evil is more than simply the lack of good (the *privatio boni* idea).

Jesus therefore gives us a much different metaphysics than the Buddha. While Chapter 4 of this book examines the evidence for the reality of disembodied consciousness (or "soul" if you will), Chapter 5 examines the implications of this for psychology, specifically as it is delineated by Christianity. In his latest book, *Lost Christianity* (1980), Jacob Needleman states:

> A fresh look at the Christian doctrine of the soul can bring us toward the cosmological element that is so lacking in modern psychology, and by implication, in the way we think about ourselves.[16]

In Chapter 5 I make the case that Jesus had knowledge of the so-called "astral plane" that far surpassed that of his contemporaries, and which is in keeping with evidence suggested by near-death and parapsychological research. The same chapter also deals with the ethical dimension of human beings, which dovetails with some near-death observations and suggests a different set of values for modern psychology to consider. Consideration is also given to the connection between Christianity as a healing religion and psychotherapy as a healing art. The name *Jeshua* means "healer of Yahweh," and Christianity, as originally preached by Jesus and the early Christians, is more healing-centered than any other major religion.

This book is intended to be a bridge between secular psychology and a large and growing literature that largely presumes that one is already a believer. The chief aim of the book is to lead the reader closer to this rich Christian literature (examples of which include Kelsey,[17] Linn & Linn,[18] and Parkhurst,[19] to name a few). At the very least, the author hopes that the reader will gain increased respect for the psychological insights of what Needleman calls "the sacred tradition" in the context of Christianity.

Another intended audience of readers are those who feel a void in their lives, and have been unable to fill it either by the various types of psychotherapy, or by the various Oriental disciplines. That there is a vacuum of meaninglessness in our society is difficult to deny. It was long hoped by many that the fulfillment of the "American dream" would satisfy everyone's needs. We are painfully finding out that that is not so. A very well-known and respected psychologist (Zimbardo, 1980) very aptly describes this emptiness that exists even among those, it would seem, for whom the American dream has become a reality:

> The children of American affluence are depicted as passively accepting a way of life that they view as empty and meaningless. The syndrome includes a constricted expression of emotions, a low threshold of boredom and an apparent absence of joy in anything that is not immediately consumable; hence the significance of music, drugs, alcohol, sex and status-symbol possessions.[20]

Zimbardo goes on to give a graphic description of young people congregating in suburban American shopping malls:

> What you witness when school is out are mass minglings of kids too young to drive, wandering about in the artificial air of a totally enclosed space amid artificial flowers, canned music, junk-food dispensers, and plastic twittering canaries.[21]

It is to those people who are tired of listening to plastic twittering canaries and who are looking for more out of life that this book is also addressed.

Notes

1. Needleman, J., *On the Way to Self-Knowledge*, J. Needleman and D. Lewis, eds. (New York: Knopf, 1976), pp. x and 23.

2. Szasz, T., *The Myth of Psychotherapy* (Garden City: Doubleday, 1978), pp. 11–24.

3. Needleman, J., *A Sense of the Cosmos* (New York: Dutton, 1975), pp. 108–109.

4. Freud, S., *Civilization and Its Discontents* (New York: Norton, 1961), p. 26.

5. Ibid., p. 89.

6. Ibid., p. 61.

7. Frankl, V., *Man's Search for Meaning* (New York: Washington Square Press, 1962).

8. Freud, S., op. cit., p. 23.

9. Moody, R., *Life After Life* (New York: Bantam, 1975).

10. Moody, R., *Reflections on "Life After Life"* (New York: Bantam, 1977).

11. Bergin, A., "Psychotherapy and Religious Values," paper presented at the Institute for the Study of Human Knowledge, New York, April, 1979.

12. McDonagh, J. "Bibliotherapy with Suicidal Patients," paper presented at the convention of the American Psychological Association, New York, August, 1979.

13. Ring, K., *Life at Death* (New York: Coward, McCann & Geoghegan, 1980), pp. 104–130.

14. Huvelin, Abbé, *Je n'aimerai jamais assez* (Paris: Fleurus, 1963).

15. Watts, A., *Psychotherapy East and West* (New York: Pantheon, 1961), pp. 12–13.

16. Needleman, J., *Lost Christianity* (Garden City: Doubleday, 1980), p. 156.

17. Kelsey, M., *Afterlife: The Other Side of Dying* (New York: Paulist Press, 1979). Kelsey, M., *Discernment* (New York: Paulist Press, 1978). Kelsey, M., *Healing and Christianity* (New York: Harper & Row, 1973).

18. Linn, M., & Linn, D., *Healing Life's Hurts* (New York: Paulist Press, 1978). Linn, M. & Linn, D., *Healing of Memories* (New York: Paulist Press, 1974).

19. Parkhurst, G., *Positive Living through Inner Healing* (Plainfield, NJ: Logos International, 1973).

20. Zimbardo, P., "The Age of Indifference," *Psychology Today*, August, 1980, vol. 14, no. 3, p. 72.

21. Ibid., p. 74.

ONE

The Confusion
about Psychotherapy

The scientific world-view, recently so full of hope, has left men stranded in a flood of forces and events they do not understand, far less control. Psychiatry has lost its messianic aura, and therapists themselves are among the most tormented by the times. In the social sciences, there exists a brilliant gloom of unconnected theories and shattered predictions.

–Jacob Needleman[1]

It has taken the West over a century to realize the futility of trying to model the social sciences on the natural and biological sciences. Auguste Comte was perhaps one of the boldest thinkers of the nineteenth century to hold forth the hope that the behavior of whole societies could be modeled after Newtonian physics. He is widely regarded as the founder of sociology, and the term he coined for it was "social physics." The psychology laboratories soon followed, with the same naive hope that finally the study of the human psyche would be freed from the speculative and nonempirical realm of philosophy and the superstitions of religion. A new day was dawning! It would not be long before human behavior could be manipulated, controlled, and predicted in order to make a better world for us all. In the same era, Darwin shocked the intellectual world and shook it to its foundations when he propounded the evolutionary theories of natural selection. Religious thinkers were appalled that anyone would trace the descent of man from some apelike creature. Some of their feeble attempts to rebut Darwin now seem quaint and pitiful, but they were painful expressions of "religious man," who felt his faith severely threatened.

The arguments against Darwin, desperate attempts to uphold revealed religion, were like sand castles trying to survive an incoming tide. I can recall reading some of these turn-of-the-century tracts in a sophomore seminar on evolution. At the time (1962), of course, the members of the seminar realized that the arguments were outdated, and that they were read for historical interest. For me it was not difficult to assimilate Darwin, and to reassess the biblical accounts of Creation in a more figurative and less literal way. What was disturbing, however, was that one of these adamantly anti-Darwinian tracts was written by a Jesuit around the turn of the century, and it now seemed so naive. My confidence in the Jesuits was shaken. Was Teilhard de Chardin (also a Jesuit) any more sophisticated in dealing with evolution, or would we look back at him as also naive?

Outside of religious circles, however, the work of Darwin and Spencer was hailed as another advance of scientific enlightenment. The view of man as a spiritual being was clearly on the defensive. But the struggle had just begun. Darwin paved the way, in a sense, for Freud. Again there were defensive reactions against his revolutionary attempt to explain human behavior in strictly biological terms. If anything, the reaction was more extreme. Unlike Darwin, Freud was explicit in his attacks on religious beliefs. Also unlike Darwin, Freud founded a brand-new science, psychoanalysis, and trained an ardent group of disciples in its methods. These were not ordinary scientists, however; they gradually abandoned the canons of modern Western science, which demanded proofs consisting of replication, prediction, and public evidence. Instead, they relied on the authority of the master. Those who disagreed with Freud were guilty of resistance, neurosis, bad faith, or all of the above. Psychoanalysis was indeed a religion, which sent forth true believers to proselytize in all parts of the civilized world. If one dissented from the master's teachings, one was ostracized or expelled. The Freudian doctrines were made obligatory with true religious fervor. Despite the heretics, the psychoanalytic disciples soon took over and became the psychiatric establishment, particularly in the United States. As they became more secure, minor modifications of the original corpus of doctrines were permitted, but significant deviations from the faith were not tolerated. We have only to witness the fate of John Bowlby, who wished to strengthen and deepen psychoanalysis as a field by investigating the phenomena of separation and loss by directly observing infants' behavior in such situations, rather than relying entirely on the recollections of childhood experiences by adult patients, which constituted the data on which psychoanalysts based their theories. It seemed like an eminently sensible thing to do. Rather than relying on the accounts given by patients (which psychoanalysis regarded as possibly distorted anyway), why not go into the nursery and have a first-hand look? Bowlby was trained as a psychoanalyst himself, and hoped that his work would enrich psychoanalysis. Unfortunately, Bowlby's observations and his interpretations did not coincide with the established tenets of psychoanalysis, and he was reprimanded by "three guardians of the psychoanalytic canon—Anna Freud, Max Shur, and Rene Spitz" (Kaplan, 1980).[2] Another example of the stir that can be caused in psychoanalytic circles when a prominent analyst tries to revise psychoanalytic doctrine can be seen in the controversy surrounding Heinz Kohut (Quinn, 1980).[3] In his attempt to introduce his "self psychology" into psychoanalysis, he has been criticized sharply by other analysts, one of whom commented that Kohut and some of his followers have an attitude "that they have brought religion to the world" (cited by Quinn, 1980). Kohut himself feels that he has been ostracized by the psychoanalytic establishment.

Erich Fromm has noted that the history of psychoanalysis has numerous examples like those mentioned above, and that it is the "bureaucracy and dogmatism" of psychoanalysis that has led to a true crisis within that field.[4] One might regard this crisis as a crisis of faith among the psychoanalytic faithful, comparable to and no less painful than that which occurred among many Christians in the wake of Darwin's and Spencer's theory of natural selection. Fromm states that there has been a decline in recent years in the number of students applying for training in psychoanalytic institutes,[5] although Quinn mentions that membership in the American Psychoanalytic Association has increased from 1975 to 1980.[6] Taken together, however, both authors agree that the number of patients applying for psychoanalytic treatment has been declining since the 1960s.

I am not suggesting that modern psychotherapy does not owe a considerable debt to Freud, who had revolutionary insights into human behavior and relationships. Many of his concepts have been corroborated by psychological research independent of the psychoanalytic tradition. For example, it was Freud who pointed out the critical importance of early childhood experiences, and their consequences on later personality development. Indeed, it was out of this tradition that John Bowlby came. However, as can be seen from the reaction of the analytic community to his findings, one gets the impression that too many analysts are impervious to, or even hostile toward, research that does not bear out psychoanalytic hypotheses. I suspect that a partial explanation of this lies in the fact that analytic institutes are sometimes closed off from the mainstream of psychological research, and the members of the analytic community support each other in their belief systems, which then become self-perpetuating. Some of the more arcane concepts of psychoanalysis are meaningless to researchers in other branches of psychology, and are likely to be meaningless to the psychological world outside the analytic office. The same criticism could be leveled at many aspects of Jungian analysis as well. Jung, however, tolerated, and even encouraged, disagreement and open debate. He was reluctant to found a school of thought for his therapeutic technique, and is reported to have said of himself, "I am not a Jungian" (Matoon, 1978).[7] A good example of how the Jungian approach is more open, while the Freudian and neo-Freudian approaches often merely mimic the teachings of the founder, is the case of transference. Transference was one of Freud's greatest discoveries. Basically, it means that patients transfer emotional, and even perceptual, reactions from parental figures onto the therapist. It is an essential ingredient of psychoanalytic therapy. In clinical circles, one hears about it all the time. It is simply assumed without question by thousands of mental health practitioners that transference is a practically universal phenomenon in therapy that is essential to its success. I am not suggesting that transference does not exist, but that it has been overused. It is possible that people interpret certain behaviors as transference because they think it must be there. Jung reports that a female patient became very upset because she was not developing a transference in her therapy with him. She had previously been in psychoanalytic therapy, and understood that transference was critical. Jung assured her that transference was not universal in therapeutic treatment, nor did he consider it essential for successful treatment. He reports that the woman was greatly relieved, and went on to a very successful treatment with him.[8] Why does the mental health community slavishly accept the psychoanalytic view of transference, while ignoring Jung, who had at least as profound an insight into human nature as did Freud? I submit that both the Freudian and Jungian schools of thought have important characteristics of a religion, but that the Freudian religion is authoritarian, while the Jungian is more democratic and allows more freedom of inquiry.

Returning to the question of disillusionment with psychotherapy, I think it is fair to say that the effects of psychotherapy, not limited to psychoanalysis, have not measured up to the expectations of the public. As evidence of this, I cite the popularity of Martin Gross's attack on the therapeutic establishment, *The Psychological Society* (1978).[9] While I take exception to most of Gross's criticisms, the popularity of his book suggests widespread disaffection with psychotherapy in general. However, self-help books are also doing a very brisk business. I believe that this is also evidence that a thirst for the needs not met by psychotherapy is widespread, and that the public hopes it can find happiness through such books.

The public has been further confused by the proliferation of many different types of therapy, from biofeedback to sensitivity groups, transactional analysis, etc. Thomas Szasz (1978) has humorously described this proliferation of therapies (including divorce therapy—in which husband and wife are considered to be "allergic" to each other).[10] It has reached the point where the meanings of the terms "therapy" and "therapeutic" have become so diluted that they have no meaning at all. "Therapeutic" has come to mean anything that makes you feel good.

In a more serious vein, professional psychologists have for some time been concerned about the confusion and disillusionment in the field of psychotherapeutic research, which is riddled with mixed and inconclusive results. A most ambitious program to evaluate and put into perspective the current findings in the field was carried out by Allen Bergin and Hans Strupp (1972).[11] Their work is probably one of the most thorough and objective contemporary works available on the status of psychotherapy.[12] It is monumental insofar as they sought to integrate the results of literally thousands of studies done in the 1950s and 60s. In addition, they interviewed over thirty of the most prominent therapists and researchers in the field, in order to incorporate the widest breadth of insight into their work.

What these men say in the epilogue of their study is most revealing. Dr. Strupp began the study with a clear preference for psychoanalytic (Freudian and neo-Freudian) approaches. He states that as a result of his joint research effort, he has become more critical of *all* (italics his) prominent theoretical formulations.[13] While giving Freud due credit for his pioneer work in the field, Strupp emphatically states that Freud "did not enunciate immutable truths, *a point still insufficiently appreciated*" (italics mine). Regarding our knowledge of the working of the human personality, Strupp states that "we are still very much in the Dark Ages." He then outlines one of the greatest obstacles to progress as *"stifling open inquiry* with the concomitant tendency to hide from ourselves the nature and extent of our ignorance."[14] My reading of this is that Strupp might as well be describing an unquestioning medieval authoritarian religion as psychotherapy, which claims so often to be a science, in which inquiry and challenge should be the name of the game.

Allen Bergin, on the other hand, began the joint project with a preference for behavioral methods, but was drawn to see the value of some psychoanalytic therapies: Some therapists clearly get good results, a proposition that Gross is loath to admit. But Bergin makes a statement remarkably similar to that of Strupp in refusing to accept any single approach as having the whole truth:

> I have found it by now completely impossible to accept any of the theoretical positions currently popular. They seem weak, superfluous and irrelevant; . . . our greatest need is for new theories. . . . Surely, the global theories that absorb the minds of the therapists and fill the pages of countless books require replacement by views that will better coordinate the facts now so abundant and confusing in the field.[15]

Dissatisfaction with current theories was experienced by both authors of a very comprehensive modern study of psychotherapy. It is of interest to note that dissatisfaction with closed theories characterized the writings of two eminent psychologists much earlier in the history of psychology: William James and Carl Gustav Jung. Both were criticized by the dominant schools of thought for being unsystematic and offering no unifying theory for psychology. James said such closure for psychology was premature. Several generations later, we find Bergin and Strupp saying the same thing concerning psychotherapy. It is of interest to note that only one therapist in the Bergin-Strupp study had Jungian training. It is of further interest to note that only Jung and James, of the most eminent psychologists, took seriously the religious dimension of human beings, and were shut out of the mainstream partly because of this. And more recently (1979), we find Bergin stating, "Religion is at the fringe of clinical psychology when it should be at the center."[16] In the early part of his career, Jung was clearly an agnostic, but toward the end of his life (1961), he was asked by a BBC commentator if he believed in God. Jung replied, "I do not believe. I know!"[17] The religious dimension of humanity permeated the writings of Jung as it did no other giant in psychology. We find Bergin and Jung converging in their thought insofar as they mistrust closed psychological theories and stress the value of religion as central in human life. How unusual it is to see such convergence of thought from very disparate backgrounds. I believe such convergence to be highly significant.

If Jung and James saw wisdom in a lack of oversystematization in psychology sixty years ago, why are Bergin and Strupp arriving at a similar position so late in the game? The reason, I believe, is that among American psychotherapists, Jung has, until recently, been *persona non grata,* and his influence eclipsed by cultural and sociological phenomena that effectively shut out his thought from American graduate schools. Although Jung labelled Nazism a "psychosis,"[18] and cited it as evidence of "naked evil" in the world,[19] some of his early, naive statements regarding it have been enough to render him for many guilty of ill will without a full hearing. There are many in the field who will not read his books for this reason.

And what of James? He was likewise ignored until recently, although lip service was given to him as the "father of American psychology." James was an embarrassment to antireligious psychologists because he took religious experience seriously and refused to pronounce it all as pathological. He also took parapsychological phenomena seriously, further limiting his influence, as logical positivism had excluded *a priori* any such experiences from its universe. It has only been very recently, on college campuses and chiefly outside psychology departments or schools of social work, that Jung and James have found a receptive audience. Several generations of logical positivist conditioning are giving way to broader views of what is real and what is unreal. The impetus is coming not chiefly from the mental health professions, but from philosophers, theologians, and physicists. It is my hope that the popularity of Jung and James among the younger generation will prompt the older generation to take their views more seriously and with an open mind.

Let us take one example of an area Jung and James probed

where positivists feared to tread: parapsychology. The mainstream of American psychology has long regarded parapsychology as some kind of illegitimate child with whom it is not respectable to associate. The psychological establishment ruled the area out of bounds, and woe to the occasional gadfly who violated the taboo. Parapsychological research in the United States has been very limited, but it receives considerable funding in the Soviet Union (Ostrander & Schroeder, 1970).[20] Whatever one may think of the Russians, they are not known to waste their rubles on trivialities. The other supreme irony here is that the realm of the parapsychological opened the door for Jung and James to the nonmaterial and the spiritual, yet a militantly atheistic and materialistic state is investigating it more than "open-minded" American academics. Could it be that our psychological establishment is afraid of something?

One might liken the three dominant forces in contemporary American psychology as corresponding to three aspects of human reality. The behaviorist school began by focusing only on concrete observable behavior (or movements); the psychoanalytic school focused on the unconscious; the humanistic (including the existential and phenomenological) approach brought back the present and consciousness as critical factors in understanding human functioning. The behaviorist school relied heavily on the findings of experimental laboratory psychology, which were based on observable movements or behaviors (usually of animals). As will be seen, when experimental psychology found it imperative to include consciousness as a variable, the nature of behavior therapy changed accordingly. Psychonalysis evolved in parallel fashion, originally considering conscious factors as relatively unimportant. All was to have an ultimate explanation in terms of unconscious processes, into which almost anything could be posited, or onto which anything could be projected. The sorely needed corrective to these schools was the humanistic, insofar as it tried to make the study of subjective conscious experience a respectable activity. All three schools, however, either implicitly or explicitly denied the existence of another order of reality, namely, the spiritual. Even Jung began as an agnostic, one who could not "believe," but had to "know." He was an incurable scientist, but dismissed by the dominant schools as a hopeless mystic.

The history of how American psychology evolved to its present state, with its prejudices and biases, would take us beyond the scope of this work. However, it would be instructive to digress briefly on the development of the behaviorist branch of psychology to see how it has abandoned some of its previously iron-clad dogmas, in a parallel manner to the way in which therapist-researchers have gradually abandoned outmoded theories. The early behaviorists wished to banish "subjectivism" forever from psychology, so that it could take its place with physics among the natural sciences. Of course, their model of physics was Newtonian, and represented a truncated segment of the physics we know today. In this process, human cognition was excluded. The founder of behaviorism, John Watson, wanted to out-do the physicists in being thoroughly objective and "scientific." There were legitimate reasons for this radical stance in psychology, as the subjectivism of Titchener and others was going nowhere.

However, in the last twenty years even the most steadfast behaviorists have realized that subjective experience cannot be arbitrarily excluded from a comprehensive psychology. Human cognition and other subjective and internal states are not only legitimate fields of inquiry, but necessary in order to provide a fuller explanation of human behavior. In transposing the results of experimental settings to the clinical one, behavior therapists such as Wolpe had to rely on data that Watson would have excluded as simply too subjectivistic. Relatively speaking, B.F. Skinner can be considered one of the positivist hold-outs. Skinner's work on the learning process has been monumental, and for that we are deeply indebted to him and to those who have applied his techniques to education. There are countless people learning things more efficiently today than they might be without this research. However, regarding the questions with which this book is primarily concerned, namely, the relationship between psychology and religion,

Skinner's theories are inadequate. With all due respect to Dr. Skinner, his philosophy seems to be based chiefly on data related to only one dimension of human experience, namely, changes in overt behavior. He has done wonders with pigeons (teaching them ping-pong, for example), but so far it has not been recorded that any pigeon has sought his personal guidance in the quest for the meaning of life. And that is probably fortunate for him and the pigeons.

In an interview on the Dick Cavett Show, Skinner gave us an interesting glimpse into the workings of his own mind, or "subjective experience." Knowing that Skinner is a strict determinist, Cavett asked him if he believed his own behavior to be entirely predetermined. Skinner replied that if he were to hold such a belief, he could not function. Rather, he seemed to hold the hypothesis that his own behavior comprised a certain amount of autonomy, or one might say, "freedom." If William James had been on the show, he would have immediately pointed out that Skinner's hypothesis of his own autonomy had pragmatic value (Skinner himself admitted as much), and would therefore be regarded as having some "truth value" in the pragmatist tradition, to which Skinner claims to belong. When one takes up a rigid *a priori* philosophical position (such as "there is no free will"), it is easy to paint oneself into a corner. Why not simply discard the position? All of us are psychologists enough to realize that the mind is not that simple. Skinner's whole system would crumble if he had replied, "Well, maybe there is such a thing as free will." As will be seen in chapter four, the phenomenon of the near-death experience raises some critical questions on the issue of "free will."[21]

It might be helpful to return to the roots of behaviorism to determine whether certain attitudes have been passed down along with the wealth of data. John Watson's exclusion of anything subjective was partly motivated by a desire to remove psychology as far as possible from religion, toward which he was quite hostile. By purging itself from subjectivism, psychology was to become free of all superstition. Religion was, *a priori*, superstition, not worthy of the *illuminati*. Scientific methodology was to replace the religious idols, and did for several generations of behaviorists. More recently, some in the field have come to see the idolatry of method as a folly traceable to Watson, and which has probably impoverished behaviorism intellectually, though yielding reams of data.

When a behaviorist studies religion, he usually focuses on religious *behavior.* This is usually limited to studying such behaviors as church attendance or observance of religious rituals. The inner religious experience, the encounter with the *other,* is still taboo as an area of investigation. Generally we do not find such studies in American psychology, unless we return to our gadfly friend, William James. The inner religious experience is the very core and heart of all religions, and can be said to give rise to the observable behaviors, such as church attendance, which may be regarded as superficial by comparison. Yet, it is this core that is simply ignored by, or forbidden to, students of religious behavior.

About the closest one comes in the behaviorist literature to studying religious experience is the study of values that can be said to derive from religion. Even here, psychologists would have been slow to explore such an area were it not for the impetus from anthropology and sociology, which did not have the methodological shackles of psychology. Psychologists are only beginning to admit that values are very important, particularly in the area of psychotherapy, but for many years this area was ignored because it was presumed that psychotherapy espoused no values.

Notes

1. Needleman, J., *The New Religions* (Garden City: Doubleday, 1970), p. 9.

2. Kaplan, L., "A Theory of Mourning," review of John Bowlby's *Loss: Sadness and Depression,* in *The New York Times Book Review,* Aug. 24, 1980, pp. 9 & 19.

3. Quinn, S., "Oedipus vs. Narcissus," *New York Times Magazine,* Nov. 9, 1980, p. 120.

4. Fromm, E., *The Crisis of Psychoanalysis* (Greenwich, Ct.: Fawcett, 1970), p. 23.

5. Ibid., p. 12.

6. Quinn, op. cit., p. 120.

7. Matoon, M., *Applied Dream Analysis* (Washington D.C.: Winston, 1978).

8. Jung, C.G., *Analytic Psychology: Its Theory and Practice* (New York: Random House, 1968), pp. 169–170.

9. Gross, M., *The Psychological Society* (New York: Random House, 1978).

10. Szasz, T., *The Myth of Psychotherapy* (Garden City: Doubleday, 1978), pp. 196–197.

11. Bergin, A., and Strupp, H., *New Frontiers in the Science of Psychotherapy* (New York: Aldine, 1972).

12. Since the initial draft of this chapter, there have appeared several extremely comprehensive studies on the effects of psychotherapy. The Office of Technology Assessment, in October, 1980, published *The Efficacy and Cost Effectiveness of Psychotherapy* (U.S. House of Representatives, Washington, D.C.). This study, in turn, reviewed other very extensive studies. Their conclusions are too detailed to delineate here, but the report certainly recognizes that there is still much controversy in this area, even after the nine years that have elapsed since the publication of the Bergin–Strupp study. For example, the work by M.L. Smith *et. al. (The Benefits of Psychotherapy,* Baltimore: Johns Hopkins Press, 1980) is seen as quite optimistic regarding the effects of psychotherapy, but the OTA study states, "Their methods (of analysis of data) are not yet widely accepted . . . ." Another comprehensive study, with more traditional approaches to data analysis, is that of M. Parloff *et. al.* ("Assessment of Psychosocial treatment of mental health disorders: current status and prospects," Report to the National Academy of Sciences, Institute of Medicine, Washington, D.C., 1978). The Parloff study examines the impact of psychotherapy on different types of disorders, and presents evidence that some forms of therapy are clearly helpful for some disorders. It is of interest to point out that neither the Smith nor the Parloff study deals at all with family therapy, a topic that will be further treated in this book. In sum, I do not believe that there is anything in the aforementioned studies that effectively contradicts the general conclusions of the Bergin–Stupp study.

13. Bergin, A. and Strupp, H., op. cit., pp. 448–449.

14. Ibid., p. 449.

15. Ibid., p. 452.

16. Bergin, A., in *Journal of Consulting and Clinical Psychology*, vol. 48, 1980.

17. Jung, C.G., in interview with Laurens van der Post, British Broadcasting Co., 1961 (on film).

18. Jung, C.G., "The State of Psychotherapy Today," from *Civilization in Transition*, cited in A. Jaffe, *From the Life and Work of C.G. Jung* (New York: Harper & Row, 1971), pp. 89–90. The entire controversy surrounding Jung's attitudes toward national socialism are treated at some length. Ms. Jaffe admits that Jung was mistaken in not seeing the evil of Nazism earlier and taking a vigorous stand against it, and even shows that Jung himself later realized this. She insists, however, that a thorough study of Jung's behavior and attitudes refutes the view that he was anti-Jewish (pp. 78–98).

19. Jung, C.G., *Memories, Dreams and Reflections* (New York: Knopf and Random House, 1961), pp. 328–329.

20. Ostrander, S., and Schroeder, S., *Psychic Discoveries Behind the Iron Curtain* (Englewood Cliffs, NJ: Prentice-Hall, 1970), p. 7.

21. A very interesting argument in defense of free will is offered by J.H. Hick, professor of theology at the University of Birmingham, England. I believe it would be a difficult one for determinists to refute: "I shall argue that we have to presume our own freedom, as minds and wills, because any claim to have rational grounds for believing that we are totally determined is necessarily self-refuting . . . . [T]he concept of rational belief presupposes intellectual freedom; so that a mind whose history is determined cannot be said rationally to believe anything or therefore rationally to believe that total determinism is true. Thus any attempt rationally to establish total determinism involves the contradiction that, in arguing for it, the mind must presume itself not to be completely determined, but to be freely judging, recognizing logical relations, assessing relevance, and considering reasons; whereas, if the determinist conclusion is true, the mind is, and always has been, completely determined and has never been freely judging." (Hick, J.H., *Death and Eternal Life*, New York: Harper & Row, 1976, p. 117).

TWO

The Myth of the Moral Neutrality of Psychotherapy

It is apparent that the so-called moral neutrality of the psychotherapist is as much a moral position as any more blatant one.

–Perry London[1]

The conventional wisdom among psychotherapists of most schools of thought is that the therapist must remain morally neutral and at all times nonjudgmental of the material related to him or her by the client. If one considers the treatment of a phobia for flying in airplanes, and the problem is tackled by means of desensitization, hypnosis, or some combination of such methods, the moral question hardly arises. However, when the client presents problems in his or her relationships with others (and this constitutes the predominant material in most psychotherapy), there is an added and unavoidable moral dimension. Questions involving sexuality, self-sacrifice vs. self-indulgence, honesty with others, etc. could all be cited as bringing us face to face with the ethical domain.

Both psychodynamic and humanistic therapies insist on the moral neutrality of the therapist on these and other questions. The psychodynamic group, for the most part, sees psychotherapy as a quasi-medical activity, and insists that no scientific practitioner should get involved with ethical values when

27

dealing with patients. (This itself is a moral position.) The humanistic therapies, while advocating similar neutrality, have a code of values of their own, including "self-actualization" and "growth," without truly grappling with the question of whether these ends may present ethical problems. For example, is it possible for a client to "actualize" his or her self at the expense of others? Although claiming to be value-free, accepting and nonjudgmental in therapy, the humanistic literature is fraught with all kinds of value judgments, for example, exalting "openness" (possibly at the expense of "tact") and freedom of sexual expression (perhaps to the detriment of commitment). Vitz deals at some length with some of the problems inherent in the humanistic therapies in his book *Psychology as Religion: The Cult of Self-Worship* (1977).[2] He regards "selfism" (the undue exaltation of the self) as a pervasive attitude in contemporary humanistic therapies, and makes passing reference to psychodynamically oriented ones as well. He also points out how this attitude has spread from the therapist's office to other areas of life. He includes a very instructive quote from Irving Kristol (1974), which points out how this position has become ensconced in the American educational establishment:

> We have a kind of faith in the nature of people that we do not have in the botanical process of nature itself—and I use the word "faith" in its full religious force. We really do believe that all human beings have a natural *telos* toward becoming flowers, not weeds or poison ivy, and that aggregates of human beings have a natural predisposition to arrange themselves into gardens, not jungles or garbage heaps. This sublime and noble faith we may call the religion of liberal humanism. It is the dominant spiritual and intellectual orthodoxy in America today.[3]

The thrust of Vitz's critique of selfism is that it is based on the naive view outlined by Kristol, and that it has been systematically reinforced in clients of humanistically oriented therapies, perhaps to the detriment of the client as well as to his or her relatives and friends. I think it is legitimate to raise the question as to whether modern psychology has not contributed to the rise of the "me generation."

The fact that "nondirective" therapy (of the Rogerian school) is not truly nondirective has been known for quite some time by academic psychologists. In the now classic study of the "Greenspoon effect" (Greenspoon, 1955),[4] it was demonstrated that subtle behaviors of the therapist could systematically "reinforce" (i.e., increase the frequency of) certain behaviors in the client in experiments conceived according to the paradigm of nondirective therapy. Such seemingly neutral behaviors as nodding approval, or showing increased interest by verbalizations such as "hmm-hmm" were shown to have a definite effect on the client. Yet the myth of neutrality persists. The evidence that the therapist's attitudes and values can be so expressed, even unconsciously, is not taken seriously.

The founder of nondirective therapy is Carl Rogers. Bergin (1979) relates a personal experience in one of Rogers's seminars wherein Rogers sought to stifle Bergin's questions and dissenting opinions.[5] Bergin concludes that if the founder of nondirective therapy is not truly nondirective, then how difficult that ideal must be for the rest of us. Again, London observes that in many situations, the therapist's not wanting to become involved in moral questions raised by the client is understandable, but the "studied attempt to avoid doing so leads the therapist into untenable positions."[6] It appears that the therapist is involved in such questions whether he or she is willing or not. It seems quite difficult to maintain that total neutrality is truly possible. And if neutrality were possible, would it not itself constitute a moral position?

Lest there be any doubt that humanistic psychology has an ethic of its own, and therefore does make value judgments, we must thank Abraham Maslow, one of the founders of humanistic psychology in the United States, for making this most explicit:

> Humanists for thousands of years have attempted to construct a naturalistic, psychological value system that could be derived from man's own nature, without the necessity of recourse to authority outside the human being himself.

Many such theories have been offered throughout history. They have all failed for mass practical purposes exactly as all other theories have failed. We have about as many scoundrels in the world today as we have ever had, and many more neurotics than we have ever had.

These inadequate theories, most of them, rested on psychological assumptions of one sort or another. Today practically all of these can be shown, in the light of recently acquired knowledge, to be false, inadequate, incomplete, or in some other way, lacking. But it is my belief that certain developments in the science and art of psychology, in the last few decades, make it possible for us for the first time to feel confident that this age-old hope may be fulfilled if only we work hard enough. (Maslow, 1962)[7]

This is quite an ambitious hope. Maslow goes on to offer a few examples of how psychological research has illustrated the wisdom of the organism, and points out how child-rearing can be improved on the basis of psychological studies. It has been nearly two decades since Maslow outlined his ambitions for the contributions from psychology toward the development of an ethical system. Whether we have progressed significantly to that end since he made the above comments, I invite the reader to judge for him or herself. Whether or not appreciable progress has been made towards the beautiful ideal Maslow holds out to us, it is my view that the concept of "human nature" that is implicit in most expressions of humanistic psychology lacks depth, and that an ethical system based on it will necessarily be inadequate. Since Maslow's death, there have been published a whole group of studies on near-death experiences (Moody,[8] Osis & Haraldsson,[9] and Ring[10]), in which I believe Maslow would have been greatly interested because they (together with some important studies from parapsychology) force us to a reappraisal of "human nature." I believe there may be implications for ethics, as well as for psychotherapy, arising from such studies. This will be explored in chapter four.

To return to Maslow briefly, he offers us a "hierarchy of values" largely based on his humanistic belief system. Related to this hierarchy, he presents us with a description of the "self-actualized" personality, which is in some respects a model of mental health (to counter the neurotic personality so often encountered in case history material by analytically oriented therapists). What is interesting here is a parallel to the litany of saints offered to us by the Christian Church as examples of what it means to be fully human. The self-actualized people he presents include Eleanor Roosevelt, Albert Einstein, and Abraham Lincoln, all admirable people to be sure. Of course, the parallel between the saints to be venerated and the self-actualized people to be admired is not complete (as most parallels are not), and some will say it is overdrawn. After all, Maslow never went about hawking statues of Albert Einstein. However, he does hold forth these self-actualized personalities as ideals, much as religions have held certain persons in high esteem, as examples of the best that human beings are capable of.

So we see that humanistic psychology does have a set of values, and therefore does sometimes make judgments. The encounter group movement, which grew out of client-centered therapy, has been compared to Protestant and Jewish pietism (Oden).[11] It's beginning to sound like psychology might be a religion as well as a science.

The idea that psychotherapy is itself a religion is not new. It is perhaps significant that psychotherapy emerged in Western culture when the traditional religions began to experience serious difficulties keeping their adherents. Psychotherapy sought to fill a religious vacuum, and it should not be surprising that it retains some of the elements of religion. Quite early in the history of psychoanalysis, Otto Rank referred to it as an "ideology."[12] The notion that psychoanalysis is more properly seen not as a science but as an ideology is very close to Szasz's recent (1979) description of psychotherapy in general as "rhetoric" rather than "science" in the Aristotelian framework.[13] If we regard psychotherapy as a form of persuasion, values would seem to be intrinsic to it.

The issue of imparting a system of values to the public is not restricted to psychotherapy alone, but extends to psychology in general. In his Presidential Address to the American Psychological Association (1975), Donald Campbell makes the following comments in this regard:

> If, as I assert, there is in psychology today a general background assumption that the human impulses provided by biological evolution are right and optimal, both individually and socially, and that repressive or inhibitory moral traditions are wrong, then in my judgment this assumption may now be regarded as scientifically wrong from the enlarged scientific perpsective that comes from the joint consideration of population genetics and social system evolution. Furthermore, in propagating such a background perspective in the teaching of perhaps ninety percent of college undergraduates (and increasing proportions of high school and elementary school pupils), psychology may be contributing to the undermining of the retention of what may be extremely valuable social-evolutionary inhibitory systems which we do not yet fully understand.[14]

It should be pointed out that Campbell is speaking in a purely secular and nonreligious frame of reference. Earlier in the address, he states, "On grounds of deep intellectual conviction, I speak from a scientific, physicalistic (materialistic) world view."[15] He identifies himself as a neo-Darwinian, and expresses some sympathy for the desire of Herbert Spencer (1879) to develop a human ethics based on science.

Historically, it should not surprise us that psychology would have its own system of values, since it emerged, in large measure, to fill a value-vacuum created by the decline of traditional belief systems. As Progoff points out:

> Psychology, one can say, was born of death, the death of old beliefs that once gave meaning to man's life. The negativity of psychology is most clearly shown in the fact that it "explains" man's beliefs—man's ancient ideologies that recur still in the modern mind—but it has no belief of its own. Psychology is capable only of explaining but not of believing.[16]

This interpretation is as provocative as it is instructive. Parenthetically, one might qualify this by asking in what sense psychology is capable of "explaining." Clearly there are organic conditions and conditioned habits that are in some sense "explainable" insofar as a cause-effect relationship between variables is fairly explicit, and capable of prediction, if not control. In this sense, we are dealing with the "scientific" (or "positivistic," if you will) aspect of psychology. When we try to find cause-effect relationships in explanations offered in depth psychology, however, we run into very complex problems. The same problem with "explanation" can be said to exist equally in the humanistic psychotherapies. In what sense is behavior in these contexts "explained"? We do not have an adequate answer to this question, unless we are willing to forego our commonly accepted view of "scientific explanation," and reason only from the explanatory system of one psychological ideology or another. It appears that a great many people have done this, and deluded themselves into thinking that behavior has been "explained." In some cases, they have bought the value systems implicit in the ideologies without realizing it.

Whether psychology is capable of "belief" is an interesting question. The rigorous experimental procedures of academic psychologists are presumed to yield a corpus of "facts" from which the applied psychologist (i.e., the therapist) may extrapolate and implement with a conviction that some kind of applied science is taking place. However, we know that all too often hard facts are not available for such application, and the therapist does not have a firm conviction that what is happening in therapy belongs in the realm of "facts" or "science." In fact, certain therapeutic techniques persist even when it has been clearly shown that they do not stand up to experimental scrutiny, or when other techniques have been shown to be superior. A good example of this can be seen in the most recent edition of Dr. Spock's baby book (1976), in which the author gives a convoluted explanation of enuresis, in the psychoanalytic model, with the suggestion of psychotherapy (presumably of a psychoanalytic orientation—since the explanation of the disorder is clearly psychoanalytic).[17] Only passing mention is made of a behavior-modification approach to the problem of enuresis, despite clear evidence that it works more quickly and with a higher success rate than traditional psychotherapy.[18] The psychoanalytic explanation of enuresis offered by Spock is pure mythology, in the most pejorative sense of the word.

In the face of this kind of bias for a method and an explanation that have failed miserably to prove themselves, one really does wonder if we are dealing with scientific facts. There are some who have observed that the process of psychotherapy can be regarded as something akin to religious conversion. The notion that clients are "converted" rather than "cured" is not entirely new. Pepinsky and Karst call the general way in which clients learn to accept the values of the therapist "convergence."[19] When convergence occurs in therapy, the client's behavior becomes more like that of the therapist. Pepinsky and Karst believe that the therapist considers the increased similarity between the client and him or herself to mean that the therapy has been successful. "Therapeutic success," therefore, is sometimes related to the value system of the therapist (or observer) and is consequently relative, and in some cases, arbitrary.

If we grant that psychotherapy, therefore, cannot be totally value-free, we must confront the implications of this. If therapy is an expression of the therapist's ideology, how should we assess it? Does the ideology stand up to logical scrutiny? How does it compare with my own ideology? We have already seen the weakness of one aspect of the humanistic ideology pointed out by Irving Kristol in the quote above. The distinction between "spiritual guide" and "therapist" becomes quite blurred, as Needleman points out:

> Spiritual guides and psychotherapists, what do your names mean? How should we accept what you call yourselves? Behind these names, which of you are the real spiritual guides and which are the real psychotherapists? We need to know. I need to know.[20]

> The shrinks are beginning to sound like gurus and the gurus are beginning to sound like shrinks.[21]

Harvey Cox's *Secular City* is in terrible trouble, as are the secular suburbs and boondocks. The high priests and seers of the secular culture are the mental health professionals, surrounded by a following of people from other professions. It may well be that the excesses of the "me generation" and the lack of personal responsibility that we see around us are bred by excessive reverence for this secular priesthood. There is, I believe, a need to demythologize the religion of psychotherapy, to challenge the authority of this priesthood, and especially to refute as false their claim to "scientific truth" about human nature. Only then will it be possible to build a new psychology, which will be free to look more deeply into human nature, casting aside the myopia of materialism. The simplistic assumptions about human nature that underlie much of social science are stultifying. The flip assertions of this or that school of thought do not do justice to the depth of human nature. The values that are espoused may well do violence to us all. Lasch (1978) summarizes the above dilemma very well when he writes:

> Therapy constitutes an anti-religion . . . because modern society has no future and therefore gives no thought to anything beyond its immediate needs. Even when therapists speak of the need for "meaning" and "love," they define love and meaning simply as the fulfillment of the patient's emotional requirements. It hardly occurs to them . . . to encourage the subject to subordinate his needs and interests to those of others, to some one or some cause or some tradition outside himself. "Love" as a self-sacrifice or self-abasement, strike the therapeutic sensibility as intolerably oppressive, offensive to common sense and injurious to personal health and well-being. To liberate humanity from such outmoded ideas as love and duty has become the mission of the post-Freudian therapies, and particularly of their converts and popularizers . . . .[22]

The philosophical and scientific assumptions of the therapeutic establishment need to be challenged.

Notes

1. London, P., *The Modes and Morals of Psychotherapy* (New York: Holt, Rinehart & Winston, 1964), pp. 11–12.

2. Vitz, P., *Psychology as Religion: the Cult of Self-Worship* (Grand Rapids, Mich: Erdmans, 1977).

3. Kristol, I., "Thoughts on Reading about a Number of Summer Camp Cabins Covered with Garbage," *The New York Times Magazine*, Nov. 17, 1964, p. 38.

4. Greenspoon, J., "The Reinforcing Effect of Two Spoken Sounds on the Frequency of Two Responses," *American Journal of Psychology*, 68, 1955, pp. 409–416.

5. Bergin, A., in *Journal of Consulting and Clinical Psychology*, vol. 48, 1980.

6. London, *op. cit.*, p. 9.

7. Maslow, A., *Toward a Psychology of Being* (New York: Van Nostrand, 1962), p. 141.

8. Moody, R., *Life After Life* (New York: Bantam, 1975).

9. Osis, K. and Haraldsson, E., *At the Hour of Death* (New York: Avon, 1977).

10. Ring, K., *Life at Death* (New York: Coward, McCann & Geoghegan, 1980).

11. Oden, T., "The New Pietism," *Journal of Humanistic Psychology*, vol. 12, 1972, pp. 24–41.

12. Rank, O., *Modern Education* (1929), cited in Progoff, I., *The Death and Rebirth of Psychology* (New York: Julian, 1956), p. 226.

13. Szasz, T., *The Myth of Psychotherapy* (Garden City: Doubleday, 1978) pp. 11–24.

14. Campbell, D., "On the Conflicts Between Biological and Social Evolution and Between Psychology and Moral Tradition," address delivered at the American Psychological Association Convention, Chicago, August, 1975, reprinted in *American Psychologist*, Dec. 1975, pp. 1103–1126.

15. Ibid., p. 1104.

16. Progoff, I., *The Death and Rebirth of Psychology* (New York: Julian, 1956), p. 221.

17. Spock, B., *Baby and Child Care* (New York: Simon & Schuster, 1976). From my own experience, Spock's ability to aid parents in diagnosing and even predicting their children's behavior is unparalleled. However, his explanations of behavior strike me as coming from an archaic era of psychoanalytic thinking.

18. Seiger, H., "Treatment of Essential Nocturnal Enuresis," *Journal of Pediatrics*, 40, June 1952, pp. 738–749.

19. Pepinsky, H.B. & Karst, T.O., "Convergence: a Phenomenon in

Counseling and Psychotherapy," *American Psychologist,* 19, 1964, pp. 333–338.

20. Needleman, J., "Psychiatry and the Sacred," in *On the Way to Self-Knowledge,* J. Needleman & D. Lewis, eds. (New York: Knopf, 1976), p. 23.

21. Needleman, J., *A Sense of the Cosmos* (New York: Dutton, 1975), p. 110.

22. Lasch, C., *The Narcissistic Society* (New York: Norton, 1978), p. 13.

THREE

Existential Psychology: A Mixed Blessing

> The ideology of personal growth, superficially optimistic,
> radiates a profound despair and resignation. It is the faith of
> those without faith.
>
> —Christopher Lasch[1]

Psychoanalysis and behaviorism had each raised hopes that the secrets and mysteries of human behavior would be understood and explained, liberating men and women from superstitions, strengthening them to see through self-deceptions and illusions, giving birth to a new utopia. Paradise lost would be regained. Depending on one's ideology, the ego would be in charge, or if one preferred behaviorism, life would be a series of positive reinforcements. Indeed, communities have been set up in an attempt to make Skinner's *Walden II* a living reality. When the long-awaited salvation by therapy and/or reinforcement did not materialize, and as critics raised questions about the scientific and philosophical truth of these systems, a new movement (or "third force") began to emerge in psychology. In Europe, it was represented by existential phenomenological psychology, while in the United States it was more often represented under the label "humanistic psychology." It is to the latter, with its emphasis on self-actualization and growth that Lasch refers above. Philosophically, however, humanistic and existential psychologies are not that far apart. Both pointed out how psychoanalysis was based on experiences with disturbed people, and thereby yielded a truncated picture of human functioning. Both affirmed the primary role played by consciousness in explaining human behavior, and correctly pointed out that behaviorism was remiss in ruling conscious experience out of bounds, while traditional psychoanalysis was equally remiss in giving undue emphasis to unconscious rather than conscious factors in human personality functioning." Both argued strongly for a holistic psychology, and alleged that behaviorism and psychoanalysis were reductionistic. Both relied on the findings of Gestalt psychology to bolster their arguments in this regard. Both rejected psychic determinism to varying degrees. Because of the rejection of deterministic explanations, both components of the "Third Force" movement were labeled as "unscientific," as if such a critique would be sufficient to silence them. The movement adopted some influential allies, such as Sartre, whose arguments for a radical human freedom were not easy to dismiss. Another ally was seen in Heisenberg, when Third Force psychologists tried to make the point that "determinism" and "science" were not coextensive and did not necessarily imply each other. Most of the humanists and existentialists were not as nihilistic as Sartre, who saw human existence as an "useless passion." The movement has been criticized as having a Pollyanna optimism about it, but that critique can probably be made of any revolution at its outset.

What seemed to inspire the humanists and existentialists more than anything was the search for meaning. They recognized quite correctly that psychoanalysis was not so much a science of facts as it was a science of interpretations. What they rejected about psychoanalysis as a system was that it subsumed practically all of human behavior into a meaning system or matrix that was artificially superimposed. Even one of the more sympathetic revisionists of psychoanalysis, Erich Fromm, states that psychoanalysis finds the ultimate explanation of human behavior in instinctual drives and needs.[2] Needleman is more direct in his critique when he writes:

> Freud thought that sexual pleasure was the most intense experience that is possible for human beings and succumbed

to constructing a whole theory of the psyche and civilization around this belief.[3]

What the existentialists wished to demonstrate was that human concerns and behaviors could not be explained or understood adequately under the rubric of sexuality, or later, aggression. Something broader was needed. One of the founders of existential psychology, Ludwig Binswanger, is quoted as writing: "Existential analysis is able to widen and deepen the basic concepts and understandings of psychoanalysis."[4] A new system of "meanings" was needed to make sense out of the myriad of data yielded by therapy with patients. Many of the existential psychologists and psychiatrists (including Binswanger) turned to the philosophy of Heidegger, who, it was felt, had articulated the most sophisticated ontological system relevant for twentieth-century western thought. It was argued with some merit by the Third Force movement that for psychology to be a viable science, it had to have a philosophical basis more suitable to it than the positivism of the nineteenth century.

What was this new vision of Heidegger's that attracted Binswanger, himself a student and lifelong friend of Freud? For Heidegger, the West had too long focused on the world of objects or beings, but had forgotten the notion of Being, which made it possible for beings to exist. Heidegger sought to elucidate the nature of Being by a thoroughgoing philosophical analysis of the *Dasein*—the only being that could reflect on its existence, and the meaning of its existence, and thereby transcend it. His method made frequent use of etymology, by which he hoped to uncover the ancient wisdom of language, through which the *Dasein* conferred meaning on its world. It was hoped that this intensive philosophical interrogation of Being would shed light on the subject–object split, which had perennially haunted philosophy and psychology. Whereas Heidegger's teacher, Edmund Husserl, had sought to purify epistemology, stripping away the excess meaning of words, and thereby get "back to the things (or beings) themselves,"

Heidegger was more radical. He wanted to illuminate the very nature of Being, without which beings could not exist.

For Heidegger and those who followed him, "meaning" was primordial. One might even paraphrase the beginning of St. John's Gospel in Heideggerian fashion to read, "In the beginning was Meaning *(logos),* and Meaning was with God, and Meaning was God." At no time, however, did Heidegger identify Being or Meaning with God, although some Christians have interpreted him in this way. For Heidegger, the *Dasein* (or "Being-in-the-World") was free to take a stance regarding its own existence, and this appealed to existential psychiatrists such as Binswanger, who saw in this a measure of human freedom. It was preferable to the psychic determinism of Freud or the behaviorists, yet not as radical as the freedom articulated by Sartre.

For Binswanger, Heidegger's system was just what psychoanalysis needed in order to become more solidly based, more credible, and truer to the human condition it sought to describe. It is vital to point out that Binswanger represents the linchpin between psychoanalysis and the existential psychologies. As has been pointed out by the French Protestant theologian, Paul Ricoeur, there are facets of psychoanalysis that are inaccessible to verification or refutation unless one has been analyzed.[5] As mentioned, Binswanger was a student of Freud and was analyzed. Equally important to point out is the fact that the two remained friends even as Binswanger began to stray from psychoanalytic orthodoxy. This is in contrast to the considerable rancor that existed when Adler and Jung went their separate ways. Freud and Binswanger always maintained mutual respect for each other's integrity; they simply agreed to disagree. And they disagreed about many things. One quote from Binswanger perhaps gets to the center of their differences. It points up Freud's contention that psychoanalysis should be ranked among the biological sciences or natural sciences, while Binswanger considered it to belong more properly to the mental sciences. This is very similar to Dilthey's distinction between the *Naturlicheswissenschaften* (physical sciences) and the *Geisteswissenschaften* (mental sciences). Binswanger wrote:

> I have not found one place in all of Freud's monumental writings where he places "the mind" *(Geist)* or "the spirit" side by side with the instincts *(Trieben)*. . . . Everywhere in his writings, human spirituality arises out of instinctuality. This is perhaps most clear where he derives the ethical from narcissism.[6]

We should consider Binswanger's dissent from Freud's biological determinism, therefore, not as the result of some personal animus, but as arising out of honest intellectual searching, and ultimately, as an honest intellectual difference.

For Binswanger, the manner in which the *Dasein* relates to its world can provide a broader view of mental health vs. mental illness. If the *Dasein* is radically open to the world *(Weltoffen)*, we have a healthy individual. If it is excessively narrowed, we have neurosis. If the *Dasein* becomes dominated by or surrenders to its own fate or instinct, we may have psychosis. Therapy is seen by existentialists as providing a meaning system to the patient that he or she did not have before. The existentialists felt that the meaning system provided by psychoanalysis was not ultimately meaningful to human beings, and was based on some erroneous assumptions about human nature. From this perspective, psychoanalysis can be seen as providing the patient with a new meaning system, which is more tolerable than the old meaning system, thereby making him or her feel better and function better. For example, the neurotic who is overcome by excessive guilt lives in a meaning system pervaded by feelings of worthlessness and self-hatred. Psychoanalysis can be viewed as a process of reeducation, whereby the patient learns to attach different meanings to events in his or her life, both intrapsychic and extrapsychic. By the subtle influence of the analyst, the patient acquires a kind of explanatory system. This system is an attempt of reason to make sense out of the irrational. Because the irrational elements in the life of a neurotic individual are in a state of turmoil, this new system provides relief. It is a very complex process in which dreams, wishes, fantasies, and behaviors all play a role. What had been fragmented and disconnected suddenly becomes coherent and makes sense. If the analysis is truly successful, these insights are usually accompanied with a great deal of affect, which had been repressed. When it is released, it no longer has as great a hold or influence on the patient's behavior. This is the phenomenon of "insight," which is common not only to psychoanalysis, but to Jungian and Adlerian approaches as well. Jung, for example, gives accounts in which the particular interpretation of a dream was accompanied by psychic relief. This was the crucial test, one might say the pragmatic truth test, of the validity of the interpretation. There is an atheoretical pragmatism in Jung, often not appreciated, which comes very close to that of William James. If it works, it's probably valid.

In the earlier days of psychoanalysis, one might say that there existed a similar pragmatism, whereby if a given interpetation appeared to alleviate the suffering of the patient, it was considered valid and became part of the foundation of the psychoanalytic method, as well as theory. As the movement progressed, however, its criteria for the "correctness" of an interpretation or a technique seemed to depend more on whether or not it fit into the basic psychoanalytic theory laid down early in its development. Moreover, a particular hypothesis might be disqualified because it violated the basically materialistic and deterministic philosophy without which psychoanalysis made no sense. This is not to say that Freud did not revise certain hypotheses. It is a matter of record that he did. But if one were inclined to make radical innovations in psychoanalytic method or theory, one usually broke formal ties with the school.[7]

In his *Will to Believe,* William James writes about the relationship between what is true and the scientific method of verification: "[Science] has fallen so deeply in love with the method [of verification] that one may even say that she has ceased to care for truth by itself at all."[8] Did Freud fall so in love with his method and theory that he ceased to care for truth? That question would take us beyond the scope of this book. However, at least one long-time observer of the psychoanalytic movement points out that many of Freud's students did not question his teachings, but merely accepted them:

> Psychoanalysis claimed to have the answer to the riddle of the human mind. It had, indeed, some "answers"—if there were such a thing in this field—to one aspect of the riddle; however, considering the vastness of the problem, there was much more that was still not understood. If the individual analyst had been aware of the fragmentary character of his knowledge—both theoretically and therapeutically—he would have felt most insecure in a situation in which even that which he did not know was rejected or ridiculed. Was it not natural, therefore, for him to support the fiction that, essentially, Freud had found the whole truth and that by magic participation he, as a member of the organization, shared in this possession of the truth?[9]

The "truth" of a given hypothesis or interpretation in psychoanalysis appears to depend on its status in the revealed corpus of teachings of the master and his followers. "Ah! But what is truth?" you will ask. One is reminded of that supremely dramatic moment in history when Pontius Pilate asked that of Jesus. If Pilate had been in analysis, he wouldn't have asked Jesus—he would have asked his analyst. While these comments are made tongue-in-cheek, I suspect the reader will recognize the situation in which patients often rely on their analysts to interpret reality for them. This critique is not limited to psychoanalysis, however, as there are therapists of other persuasions who seem to think they have a truer picture of reality than the rest of us.

"We all have *some* truth," wrote Paul Ricoeur. It is when a partial truth is made into a total truth that we become "totalitarians of the mind." In Barrett's words:

> We have imprisoned ourselves in a total ideology beyond which we cannot see. We are no longer free to let things be what they are, but must twist them to fit into the framework we impose. Yet we ourselves have freely chosen to surrender this freedom. Why? Because, like children afraid of the

dark, we cannot abide to stand within mystery, and so must have a truth that is total.[10]

This is more or less the objection made by phenomenologists to the status of modern science and philosophy, and psychoanalysis in particular. In his *Crisis of European Sciences and Psychology* (1935), Husserl singles out psychology as having a peculiar crisis of its own: the enigma of subjectivity, the enigma of psychological subject-matter and method:

> Can reason and that-which-is be separated where reason, as knowing, determines what is? . ﹏. Thus the crisis of philosophy implies the crisis of all modern sciences as members of the philosophical universe.

Husserl's primary effort was to develop an epistemology, or theory of knowledge, that would be able to buttress philosophy as the central science, upon which other sciences would rest. He was concerned chiefly about what is true. Indeed, his mission was to establish a philosophy of what is irrefutably or apodictically true. This new philosophy would be the cornerstone of all modern science. Some in the phenomenological movement have taken Husserl's insights on intentionality (the act of giving meaning or signifying) and "totalized" them into a new ideology, which, like psychoanalysis before it, determines what is true by whether or not a given hypothesis is in agreement with Husserl or other leading phenomenologists. Such proponents of phenomenological psychology would be quite shaken to learn that three years before his death in 1938, having fallen into despair, Husserl wrote, "Philosophy as a science, a serious, rigorous and indeed apodictically rigorous science—*the dream is over.*"[12] This situation, however, has not stopped some phenomenologists and existentialists from dreaming on. This is not to say that phenomenology has not been valid and useful, only that it should not purport to offer the only valid approach to psychology.

Perhaps it can be seen from the foregoing why the title of this chapter refers to existential psychology as a "mixed blessing." Despite its ultimate shortcomings, it opened up psychology beyond the narrow limits of behaviorism and psychoanalysis. Barrett's treatment of Husserl's mission is most relevant here. Husserl was particularly concerned that psychology would assimilate itself into a clumsy imitation of what goes on in the physical sciences. Barrett writes:

> [Psychology's] researches go off in all directions but lack a unifying center. The situation has become, if anything, more aggravated since Husserl wrote. Discoveries upon discoveries have piled up, but the unifying conceptions seem lacking. And the rate of discovery seems constantly accelerating. Each decade knows immensely more than the preceding, and seems just that much more confused than its predecessor.[13]

Husserl bravely sought to end this confusion, to reassert the primacy of reason, and thereby restore a measure of certainty to searching Western men and women. Ultimately he failed, and he admitted it. Deeper than this, however, is his basic premise, given in the beginning of *The Crisis of European Sciences and Psychology* (1935), which set important limits to his work and that of his followers, who established existential and phenomenological psychologies traceable to him. Husserl wrote, "It is reason which ultimately gives meaning to everything that is thought to be, all things, values and ends."[14] It is the author's contention that this is a serious fallacy, and herein lies one of the chief shortcomings of Husserl's phenomenology, which fallacy is reflected in the existential psychology of Binswanger. To contend that reason *ultimately* gives meaning to *everything* takes considerable hubris. It further precludes a truly radical openness to the possibility that some important meaning in the universe comes not from reason, and ultimately, not from human beings. It shuts us off from seeing validity in ways of human knowledge that do not conform to "reason" (such as intuition and knowledge gained by mystical experience). It further precludes that meaning might come from beyond physical reality, and from beyond human sources. In other words, it neglects to take seriously the possibility that meaning in the universe might be grounded in the Other, and therefore might be found in what we call "revelation." Sadler (1969) points out that Binswanger rejected "any sort of theological answer to the question of man's meaning," and may have discovered thereby a problem that phenomenology cannot answer. In short, the limitation of "meaning" to "human meaning" is why existential psychology is not adequate to the task of establishing the basis of a Christian psychology. Its primary virtue lies in its unmasking the illusions of psychoanalysis and behaviorism.

Lest one think that this objection to the shortcomings of phenomenology is trivial, let us look at the personal views of another great thinker who found his own philosophy likewise unable to quench the thirst for meaning. Ludwig Wittgenstein was one of the most brilliant proponents of the school of linguistic analysis. Barrett tells us that when Wittgenstein served in World War I, he picked up a copy of Tolstoy's version of the New Testament. In an essay that accompanies Tolstoy's translation is the sentence: "The more we live by our intellect, the less we understand the meaning of life."[15] Barrett writes that for Wittgenstein, the meaning of the world lies outside the world; "Consequently, the striving of the will, so far as it is engaged with this meaning, is pointed beyond the world." According to Barrett, Wittgenstein told his publisher that the unwritten part of his work is more important than what he has written.[16]

Another surprise comes from Wittgenstein's view of ethics. Although Wittgenstein does not give us his own system of ethics, it is clear that his ethics are not naturalistic or utilitarian, unlike what one might expect from a proponent of a very naturalistic philosophical school. "The ultimate good [for Wittgenstein] could not be defined finally and completely as happiness or the greatest balance of pleasure over pain."[17]

Modern Western psychology, as a whole, preaches an ethics of pleasure. The road to self-actualization (referred to by Lasch) is chiefly pleasure-oriented. Furthermore, it is pleasure for the self, and only incidentally, pleasure for others. The "good" as distinct from the "pleasureable" is practically never discussed by contemporary psychology, usually on the grounds that such discussions are not proper in a science, and belong in philosophy or theology. But there is an ethic implicit in psychology nonetheless. As a field dealing with human behavior, how could this be otherwise? In this regard, Lasch cites Rose, who maintains that the psychoanalytic outlook "inappropriately transplanted from analytic practice to everyday life" has contributed to "global permissiveness" and "over-domestication of instinct," which, in turn, contributes to the proliferation of "narcissistic identity disorders."[18] But who is to say what is appropriate and what is not in "transplanting" the psychoanalytic outlook to everyday life? Is it possible that the psychoanalytic outlook itself might foster narcissism? (I use the term "narcissism" here in the popular sense of being turned in on oneself; professionals seem to disagree anyway on a single definition of narcissism).

One corrective to being morbidly concerned with the self (often without considering the feedback system that the self has with others) has been family therapy. Here again, blind adherence to Freudian doctrine retarded the advance of psychotherapy. An internationally renowned family therapist (Napier, 1978) writes:

> In turning away from the family, Freud took generations of therapists with him. Or rather, they followed him. How could so many otherwise able therapists avoid seeing the profound implications which the family has in the lives of their patients? They have betrayed Freud's sense of quest and inquiry by following his example so slavishly, for so long, and with so little question.[19]

More will be said of family therapy later, but let us return to the discussion of existential psychology and its relationship to ethics. What, if anything, does existential psychology have to offer that is different from the pleasure principle? Generally, one does not read of a radically different ethic in existential psychology, despite the fact that it is very self-consciously grounded in philosophy, and most philosophical systems grapple with ethics at some point. In fairness, however, Rollo May discusses what could be regarded as the beginnings of an ethical system in his book *Love and Will*.[20] In this discussion he brings us back to Heidegger and the latter's treatment of the concept of *care (Sorge)*. May's treatment of care is very enlightening and helpful in enabling us to understand one of Heidegger's central concepts. May extrapolates from Heidegger to relate care to psychotherapy. In this context, a good therapeutic relationship is characterized by care on the part of the therapist for the client, in the sense of wishing him or her well.

May mentions the relationship Heidegger saw between care and conscience, but does not explore it further.[21] One must return to the text of Heidegger himself to appreciate how this relationship might relate to ethics:

> The call of conscience—that is, conscience itself—has its ontological possibility in the fact that *Dasein*, in the very basis of its Being is care.

> So we need not resort to powers with a character other than that of *Dasein;* indeed, recourse to these is so far from clarifying the uncanniness of the call (of conscience) that instead it annihilates it.[22]

Heidegger goes on say that so-called "explanations" of conscience have gone "off the track."[23] In the clearest possible terms, Heidegger is asserting that the conscience cannot be reduced or explained away. It is primordial. It is an essential experience of Being-in-the-World. Heidegger's philosophy is decidedly not theology, and one does not wish to put words into his mouth, but it is hard to resist comparing the above passage to one in St. Paul's Epistle to the Romans (2:14–16), in which he refers to the Law of God being "written in the hearts" of those who do not know the Law. The central point being made in both texts is that conscience is a universal human phenomenon, even though the contexts of the two discussions are quite different. I am not suggesting that we accept Heidegger's assertion without question. There is a fair amount of empirical data that runs counter to it. I believe, however, that these data could be reassessed with a view toward redefining what we mean by "conscience," and simply raise the question as to whether empirical research has done this sufficiently.

Of course, the mere assertion of the primordial existence of conscience in the human experience is very far removed from the delineation of an ethical system that one encounters in the more classical philosophical systems, let us say, of Kant or Aristotle. But it is a bold statement for a twentieth-century Western philosopher to make. It does come close to what might be regarded as traditional Christian psychology, before psychology broke away from philosophy in the nineteenth century. The parallels between Heidegger's philosophy and the religious theme of salvation is pointed out succinctly by Barrett (1978):

> [Heidegger's philosophy] has almost the elements of a plot or story about it. And this story, oddly enough in a work so austerely secular in tone, follows the outlines of the traditional religious tale of salvation. Heidegger tells us how our human being, thrown into the world, may lose itself there, and sink to a fallen state; but how through the encounter with conscience, anxiety and death, it is called to and can become an authentic self. But if Heidegger follows the outlines of a religious parable of salvation, what he finally offers is at the farthest remove from the usual consolations of religion. The encounter with anxiety and death opens up no heavenly perspectives for the self. It discovers in that encounter only its own nothingness.[24]

In terms of trying to build a Christian psychology, what we get from Heidegger and those who borrowed from him (such as Binswanger), to extrapolate to psychology, is a mixed bag. On the one hand, we have an inspiring view of what it means to be human: the ability to transcend one's fate in taking a stance toward it. Human faculties such as freedom and conscience are resurrected in a new way, but they are not resurrected very long, for the ultimate Heideggerian freedom is freedom toward death. It is for precisely this reason that the author views the existential psychologies derived from Heidegger as, pardon the pun, a "dead end." When Heidegger wrote, the Christian view of an afterlife was taken seriously by almost no one in academic circles in the West. In the interest of completeness and fairness to Heidegger, however, it should be pointed out that he did not deny the possibility of the survival of the personality, but neither did he affirm it. Since that time, there has accumulated a very important literature that is supportive of the survival of the human personality in an afterlife. It is a literature that offers much more hope than is offered by "post-Christian" theologians, such as Paul Tillich, who regarded immortality as living in the memory of God. This literature on the afterlife comes from decidedly nonreligious sources, and challenges psychology to return to its own etymology. In other words, the notion of *psûche* (as "soul") can no longer be avoided by twentieth-century Western psychology, but must be dealt with as it was at the time of Plato, albeit with new insights and methods developed since then. From the time of the Enlightenment until the third quarter of the twentieth century, such a proposition would be regarded as absurd. I submit that it is not absurd, but necessary if psychology is to become a more complete study of the human person. An examination of the evidence for the existence of the survival of death of the human personality, therefore, is the next step.

Notes

1. Lasch, C., *The Narcissistic Society* (New York: Norton, 1978), p. 51.

2. Fromm, E., *The Crisis of Psychoanalysis* (Greenwich, CT: Fawcett, 1970), p. 138–142.

3. Needleman, J., *A Sense of the Cosmos*, pp. 125–126.

4. Binswanger, L., "The Case of Ellen West: An Anthropological-clinical Study," in *Existence*, Rollo May, ed. (New York: Simon & Schuster, 1958), p. 315.

5. Ricoeur, P., *De l'interprétation: essai sur Freud* (Paris: Editions du Seuil), 1965, pp. 337–380.

6. Binswanger, L., *Being-in-the-World* (New York: Basic Books, 1968), p. 184.

7. Fromm, E., op. cit., pp. 12–41.

8. James, W., *The Will to Believe* (New York: Longmans-Green, 1937), cited in McDonagh, J., "The Open-ended Psychology of William James," *Journal of Humanistic Psychology*, vol. 13, no. 3, Summer, 1973, p. 52.

9. Fromm, E., op. cit., p. 23.

10. Barrett, W., *The Illusion of Technique* (Garden City: Double-day, 1978), p. 150.

11. Husserl, E., "The Crisis of European Sciences and Psychology," address delivered at Prague, 1935 (trans. by D. Carr), in *Transcendental Phenomenology* (Chicago: Northwestern University Press, 1970), pp. 11–12.

12. Husserl, E., cited in Barrett, W., op. cit., p. 125.

13. Barrett, W., op. cit., pp. 121–122.

14. Husserl, E., op. cit., p. 13.

15. Wittgenstein, L., cited in Barrett, W., op. cit., p. 31.

16. Wittgenstein, L., cited in Barrett, W., op. cit., p. 55.

17. Barrett, W., op. cit., p. 53.

18. Rose, G., cited by Lasch, C., op. cit., 1978, pp. 42–43.

19. Napier, A., (with Whitaker, C.), *The Family Crucible* (New York: Bantam, 1978), p. 42.

20. May, R., *Love and Will* (New York: Norton, 1969), pp. 290–291.

21. Ibid., p. 290.

22. Heidegger, M., *Being and Time,* J. Macquarrie and E. Robinson, translators (New York: Harper & Row, 1962), pp. 322–323.

23. Ibid., p. 323.

24. Barrett, W., op. cit., p. 139.

FOUR

Metaphysics and Psychology: The Case for an Afterlife

We are such stuff
As dreams are made on; and our little life
Is rounded with a sleep.
                        The Tempest IV: i.

But that the dread of something after death,
The undiscovered country, from whose bourn
No traveller returns, puzzles the will,
And makes us rather bear those ills we have,
Than fly to others that we know not of.
                        Hamlet III: i.

Which of these passages contains the more accurate insight about human nature? The conventional wisdom of modern psychology would almost certainly side with Prospero in *The Tempest,* and if the brooding Prince of Denmark could make his way to a modern therapist's office, his "dread" would just as certainly be viewed as groundless. If his case were to be judged as acute, he might even be given a prescription for an antidepressant. The reason for this, of course, is that contemporary Western psychology and psychiatry have ruled the study of the possibility of post-death existence of the human personality as out of bounds, because to do so would necessitate a concept of something akin to a soul or spirit. In launching behaviorism, John Watson quite emphatically equates belief in the soul with superstition.[1] That pretty much set the tone for American psychology for the next several generations. Watson, of course, was only one of many who were conditioned by an intellectual environment of radical materialism. And, so the *psûche* (or soul), by etymological definition, the object of study of psychology and psychiatry, was presumed by both sciences not to exist. Most of us (myself included) have been conditioned by this all-pervasive materialistic frame of reference, which constitutes a considerable deterrent to believing in the existence of a soul. In a fairly recent European survey, Delooz found that one Christian out of three declares that he or she is a convinced Christian, without having any certainty as to the reality of a personal life after death.[2] Until recently I would have placed myself in that category.

What turned around my thinking on this question, as mentioned in the Introduction, was Raymond Moody's *Life After Life*[3] and the subsequent readings prompted by it. Because we do live in a scientific age, we are more likely (most of us) to be persuaded (if we are persuaded at all) by a work that is presented in a dispassionate manner, and based on unbiased accounts, by an author that seems to have no axe to grind. Such is the character of Moody's work, and as such, I believe, it has rendered an invaluable service to psychology. It is a major watershed in the history of psychology, because of the controversy it has already sparked, and because it obliges psychologists once again to take seriously the phenomenon of a disembodied human personality. It thereby raises questions of metaphysics, as well as ethics, and forces us to think in a new way about free will.

Moody makes very clear, and he is very careful on this point, that his findings do not constitute a scientific or philosophical "proof" of the independent existence of the human personality after death. However, at the conclusion of his accounts of the near-death experiences of the people interviewed, he makes a statement that, I believe, goes directly to the central question at issue here:

At the same time, it seems to me to be an open possibility that our present inability to construct a "proof" may not represent a limitation imposed by the nature of the near-death experiences themselves. Perhaps it is instead a limitation of the currently accepted modes of scientific and logical thought. It may be that the perspective of scientists and logicians of the future will be very different. (One must remember that historically logic and scientific methodology have not been fixed and static systems, but growing, dynamic processes).[4]

Moody is not alone in this assessment. Referring also to experiences of clinical death and near-death, Grof and Grof (1980) state:

The possibility of consciousness after death was rejected not because it contradicted clinical observations, but *a priori* because the concept was incompatible with existing scientific theories. However, the paradigms in science should not be confused with reality or truth; at best they represent working models that organize existing observations. When they cannot account for and accommodate scientific data of major significance, they have to be replaced by more adequate conceptual frameworks.[5]

Are our notions of "science" and "scientific proof" unduly limiting, as Moody and the Grofs suggest? Such a question provokes serious concern (perhaps even anxiety) among professional scientists. In the case of Western psychology, committed to a worldview of materialism and determinism, the data collected in near-death experiences are especially anxiety-provoking. They may require a complete overhaul of the entire discipline. One ought therefore, to be on the lookout for those committed to that worldview, that they don't succumb to invoking Murphy's Law: "If your data don't conform to your theory, throw out your data." If demonstrated, the implications of the existence of a nonmaterial human personality surviving death may suggest to modern therapists that much of their lives' professional activity could be based on a seriously flawed set of assumptions about the human personality. Such a realization might be akin to the "crisis of faith" of the disillusioned religious believer.

Another reason for concern in the scientific community is the prospect that if the validity of current scientific assumptions is seriously called into question, many impressionable people will react against science, and will be prompted to give greater credence to the pie-in-the-sky sensationalistic claims of a whole host of counterculture types including mediums, parapsychologists, self-serving gurus, and ultimately, the *National Enquirer.* Such a prospect might give rise in the committed scientist to something akin to "existential despair." Is this what Paul Tillich meant by *The Shaking of the Foundations?*[6]

To rescue science from this dismal prospect comes an author who presents us with a slightly less radical alternative than Moody's questioning of the limits of "accepted modes of scientific and logical thought." Kenneth Ring has provided us with a superb extension of Moody's work, and he likewise approaches his subject matter in a dispassionate manner.[7] Like the Grofs, he alludes to the notion that a paradigm shift in science may already be underway, prompted not only by data on near-death experience, but also findings in parapsychology. However, he makes full use of the scientific methods presently available in psychology to scrutinize and analyze the near-death data. I think we should follow his analyses of the data carefully, because they effectively refute a number of the traditional materialistic attempts to dismiss the significance of the near-death phenomena that have begun to emerge, such as Siegel.[8]

For those who are not familiar with the literature on near-death phenomenona, it might be helpful to give a brief description of it before further discussion and analysis. Moody gives us a composite picture of the various aspects of the phenomenon. By no means do all near-death experiencers report all of these elements, but the composite picture represents the common elements most often found. It should be noted that the composite picture given to us by Moody is essentially similar to that found by several other investigators working independently of him (Osis & Haraldsson,[9] Rawlings,[10] Ring[11]).

A man is dying and as he reaches the point of greatest physical distress, he hears himself pronounced dead by his doctor. He begins to hear an uncomfortable noise, a loud ringing or buzzing, and at the same time, feels himself moving very rapidly through a long dark tunnel. After this, he suddenly finds himself outside of his own physical body, but still in the immediate physical environment, and he sees his own body from a distance, as though he is a spectator. He watches the resuscitation attempt from this unusual vantage point and is in a state of emotional upheaval.

After a while he collects himself and becomes accustomed to his odd condition. He notices that he still has a "body," but one of a very different nature and with very different powers from the physical body he has left behind. Soon other things begin to happen. Others come to meet and help him. He glimpses the spirits of relatives and friends who have already died, and a loving, warm spirit of a kind he has never encountered before—a being of light—appears before him. This being asks him a question, nonverbally, to make him evaluate his life and helps him along by showing him a panoramic, instantaneous playback of the major events in his life. At some point he finds himself approaching some sort of barrier or border, apparently representing the limit between earthly life and the next life. Yet, he finds that he must go back to the earth, that the time for his death has not yet come. At this point he resists, for by now he is taken up with his experiences in the afterlife and does not want to return. He is overwhelmed by intense feelings of joy, love and peace. Despite his attitude, though, he somehow reunites with his physical body and lives.

Later he tries to tell others, but he has trouble doing so. In the first place, he can find no human words adequate to describe these unearthly episodes. He also finds that others scoff, so he stops telling other people. Still, the experience affects his life profoundly, especially his views about death and its relationship to life.[12]

There are a number of traditional scientific explanations of the above set of events, all or most of which have been found inadequate by near-death investigators themselves (Moody, Osis & Haraldsson, Rawlings, and Ring). In proceding, I will refer mostly to Ring's work, because it is the most recent, and because after his refutations, Ring offers his own speculations in the form of what might be called nontraditional scientific hypotheses with which I wish to dialogue.

In the world of clinical psychology and psychiatry, perhaps the most frequent explanation of the above phenomena offered is that of depersonalization. It is essentially a psychoanalytically derived view in which the dying person, either consciously or unconsciously wishing to deny his or her imminent death, becomes psychologically detached. A psychological mechanism comes into play to defend the self against the unacceptable reality of the apparently imminent death. Ring effectively refutes this interpretation in pointing out that sometimes (if rarely), the near-death survivor reports seeing a deceased relative who was not known to be dead at the time of the near-death experience.[13] He refers to Kübler-Ross[14] who has also reported this, as well as Bayless[15] and Hyslop.[16] In addition, he could have cited a personal communication from Moody in which a dying woman met in the so-called tunnel a friend whom she believed to be alive, but who, it was subsequently learned, suffered a cardiac arrest at approximately the same time.[17] In addition to this, one could cite instances related by other investigators, in which near-death survivors reported events taking place at the scene of their near-death, or at some distance from it, while they were presumed dead, and which were later verified to have taken place as they described (Rawlings,[18] Fiore & Landsburg,[19] Lundahl[20]). Incidents of this type have also been found in "out-of-body experiences" not related to imminent death (Monroe,[21] Tart[22]). If this were not enough to refute the depersonalization interpretation, Ring also describes "paranormal knowledge of the future." In one of these cases, a woman saw two children whom she experienced as her own during the near-death experience, but whom she did not have until several years later. In another case, a man stated that he was told during his near-death experience that he should not commit suicide because his girlfriend and family members cared for him, and included in these was a daughter who was not yet born.[23] Another such experience is described by Moody.[24]

Other psychological explanations include wish-fulfillment,

psychological expectations, dreams, and hallucinations. The above objections to psychological detachment apply equally to these. In addition, Ring cites Kübler-Ross, who states that children who have these experiences never report seeing living parents, which would be expected in terms of any of these psychological explanations. They always report dead relatives or religious figures.[25] Others report seeing a dead relative never seen in life (Ring,[26] Lundahl[27]). The "psychological expectation" explanation cannot account for the fact that most of the experiencers report scenes of the afterlife that are at considerable variance from what might have been expected, given their religious and cultural background.

There are another set of explanations that are medical in nature. These include effects presumed to result from anesthetics or other drugs. In addition to being unable to account for the paranormal knowledge discussed above, Ring and others have observed that, if anything, drugs (such as those ingested by the would-be suicide) tend to dull the whole experience and reduce its vividness.[28] Also, many of the near-death experiencers had no anesthetic or drug at the time of the experience. Noyes and Kletti have offered an explanation of the panoramic playback of one's past as resulting from a seizure-like neural firing pattern in the temporal lobe.[29] Moody, himself a psychiatrist, observes that such temporal lobe firing does not usually result in memory images played back in an orderly fashion, nor are such flashbacks "seen at once in a unifying vision."[30] Also, seizure victims typically do not remember their flashbacks after regaining consciousness.

Another medical explanation that has been offered is that of cerebral anoxia, or reduced oxygen supply to the brain. Moody fields this explanation by saying, "I have dealt with some near-death experiences in which no apparent clinical death took place, and these contain many of the same features as those in which there was such a 'death.' "[31] Other medical explanations are dealt with by Ring, including the possible release of endorphins (the body's own opiate), which could account for the release from physical pain and the feelings of peace. Ring leaves the door open for more sophisticated neurological explanations (including endorphins), but cautions that such explanations will have to account not merely for one or two aspects of the near-death experience, but for the total range of phenomena grouped under this experience. I would go a step further and venture to say that the endorphin explanation certainly could never account for the paranormal knowledge (discussed above), and it is hard to conceive that anything in traditional neurology could explain that aspect of the experience.[32]

In addition to the glimpses of paranormal knowledge presumably gained while out of the body, there is a particularly noteworthy experience described by Moody, in which a man who was trapped in a vat of hot acid, and who felt the acid burning him through his clothing, heard a voice urging him to follow it. His eyes were closed throughout the ordeal (as shown by the fact they did not need treatment from exposure to the acid). Although he "knew" there was no way out of the vat, he followed the voice, eyes closed, and survived. Had he turned in any direction but that indicated to him by the voice and the accompanying bright light, he states that he would have been killed instantly. During the experience, the man recalled a verse from Scripture which, he states, had not meant much to him up until that time. The passage was the phrase spoken by Jesus to his disciples after the Resurrection and prior to the Ascension: "I am with you always" (Matthew 28:20). The man stated that he had not been very religious before this, but his attitude was changed by the experience. He stated that he crawled "some forty to fifty feet" through the burning acid to safety. It is not likely that a hallucinating man would have survived this ordeal. The man himself gives it an unequivocally spiritual interpretation, which in this case, is Christian. Moody gives other examples of "rescue" experiences, which are less dramatic, but also religious, as interpreted by the persons who were saved.[33]

Let us not, however, jump to conclusions. There is at least one nonmaterialistic yet nonreligious interpretation of these and related data that has been offered by Ring.[34] Before dealing with his interpretation, however, I think it would be useful at this juncture to put into perspective the near-death experience from a frame of reference offered by the discipline of theology. John Hick, professor of theology at the University of Birmingham, England, offers a distinction between "eschatology" (which is the study of the last or ultimate state) and "pareschatology" (which is a picture of what happens between death and the ultimate state).[35] Near-death experiences would appear to be classified in the category of "pareschatology," since they do not reflect what might be the nature of things in the "ultimate state." Indeed, there are many who would question whether there is such a thing as an ultimate state, and who would suggest that everything (including ourselves) is in a state of perpetual flux and transformation. We obviously have no scientific or quasiscientific data that can answer such a proposition either negatively or positively. I introduce Hick's distinction here because I think it would be premature for anyone to interpret what happens in the near-death experience as constituting their final fate. That knowledge is simply not given to us by such phenomena.

Let us now return to the very important interpretation of the near-death experience by Kenneth Ring. I believe his work represents a serious attempt to keep the explanation of these experiences under the general rubric of "scientific." This, indeed, is (or has been) a chief function of psychology, namely, to offer naturalistic explanations of phenomena that might be too readily explained by the "supernatural." (The categories "naturalistic" and "supernatural" might be entirely arbitrary, but that is what Western science conceives, so as to mark itself off from "nonscientific" fields such as religion). Indeed, the whole thrust of post-Enlightenment intellectual activity has been in the direction of giving naturalistic explanations to phenomena previously assumed to have supernatural explanations. I believe most readers will share the bias that a phenomenon ought to be thoroughly examined for possible naturalistic explanations before invoking a supernatural explanation, which runs the risk of being arbitrary, unverifiable, and/or superstitious. It may come as a surprise to some readers that the Catholic Church shares this bias, and requires that

alleged supernatural events (e.g., miracles, visions, possessions) be thoroughly and rigorously investigated by qualified
professionals before a supernatural explanation will be taken
seriously.

Having examined various materialistic explanations of a
more traditional scientific tenor (as outlined above), Ring re-
jects them and is left with the conviction that in the near-
death experience we are dealing with a "disembodied consciousness."[36] This accounts for the subjective sensations of
lightness of weight and the absence of physical pain, which
have also been observed to occur in out-of-body experiences.[37]
In one such study, a woman who could "leave her body" at will
was monitored on an electroencephalograph.[38] Experts who
examined her brain waves while she was "out" could not identify her readings by any known sleeping or waking pattern.
These results have been replicated by Tart[39] and by Osis.[40]
Furthermore, it has been shown that persons who can leave
their bodies are able to either "float up" short distances
(Tart[41]), or project themselves at longer distances (study by
Osis, cited in Greenhouse[42]) and report in precise detail spe-
cified visual "targets" (in one case, a five-digit number, in
another, an arrangement of toy furniture). Hence, the first
part of the explanation of the near-death experience, as offered by Ring, is derived from the findings of parapsychology.[43]
Of course, the materialistic scientists as well as parapsychologists have quite some difficulty in explaining by what mechanism these feats are possible. Some readers may feel that
modern physics just hasn't caught up with these findings, so
that they might be explained by concepts of physics that haven't been developed yet. In other words, from the perspective of a physicalistic notion of the world, a parapsychological
"explanation" is not necessarily an explanation at all. It may,
in fact, just beg the question.

There is another aspect to the near-death phenomenon and
out-of-body experiences that should be examined. This is the
"second body of some kind" that a minority of Ring's subjects
reported as detaching itself from the physical body. This has
been noted to occur with varying frequency in other near-

death studies (Moody,[44] Osis & Haraldsson,[45] Rawlings[46]), as well as in out-of-body experiences (several are cited by Currie[47]). There are a number of examples cited by Ring in which this "double" was perceived to some extent by witnesses.[48] Pushing this idea a little further, experimenters on out-of-body experiences tried to determine whether animals could detect the presence of a person who was adept at projecting consciousness out of his body. At the University of North Carolina, Morris asked this subject to project his consciousness into the cages of four animals: a gerbil, a hamster, a snake, and a cat. Only the snake and the cat displayed a reaction.[49] Besides making a good Halloween reading, this study prompts one to wonder why snakes and cats figure so prominently in supernatural legends, in contrast to gerbils and hamsters. Who ever heard of a gerbil having nine lives? Or St. Patrick driving the hamsters out of Ireland? At this writing, I am not aware that this study has been replicated, and therefore would take it with a grain of salt.

What can be taken more seriously, however, are the experiences cited by several authors above, wherein people perceive their own "double." What is this double made of? How long does it continue to exist apart from the physical body? These are questions that cannot yet be answered scientifically. If the double (or "astral body") has some characteristic (whether particles or energy) that can be measured in some way, then maybe (and this is a very big "maybe") we can understand how it can sometimes be perceived by others, but more importantly, how it generally (in the above accounts) is capable of visual and auditory perception itself. If it disappears after a period, while disembodied consciousness continues, then by what mechanism does this disembodied consciousness perceive the visual and auditory events of the near-death experience? Ring states clearly, "I do endorse the proposition that consciousness (with or without a second body) may function independently of the physical body."[50]

The functioning of the disembodied consciousness is explained by Ring in terms of parapsychology. That this "explanation" may merely beg the question, I think, is most clearly demonstrated by the work of the Soviet parapsychologist, Vasiliev.[51] He hoped to show that ESP was caused by "brain radiations." Rogo gives the account as follows:

> In Vasiliev's experiments, the agent and percipient were separated by the use of a Faraday cage, an apparatus that grounds any electromagnetic waves. Vasiliev's theory was that this shielding would immediately halt ESP, and would of course demonstrate the physical nature of ESP and show that it is a normal and measurable force. Much to his chagrin, the Faraday cage had no effect on ESP and successful results were achieved despite it.[52]

His results prompted parapsychologists to speculate that sub-atomic particles were involved, or that a mysterious force known as "psi" would explain ESP. But these explanations really don't explain anything in terms of the physical-energy world as we know it. I think it is important to stress this before proceding to Ring's explanation of the second phase of events in the near-death experience.

Ring believes that it is possible to explain the events of the near-death experience in terms of the theory and findings in the relatively new field of holography.[53] He quotes one of the leading researchers in holography to support his contention that mystical experiences from a variety of religious traditions can be interpreted in the light of holography:

> It seems to me that some of the mystical experiences people have described for millenia begin to make some scientific sense. They bespeak the possibility of tapping into that order of reality (that is, holographic reality) that is behind the world of appearances.[54]

Just what is holography, and how can it be said to explain mystical and near-death experiences? To answer this question thoroughly would take us into the field of optics and the physical explanation of the hologram. For our purposes, however, I believe it is sufficient to understand that holography is basically a relatively recent method of photography that does not require the use of lenses. Ring gives a brief synopsis, which I quote:

In holography, the wave field of light scattered by an object —say, an orange—is recorded on a plate as an interference pattern. The idea of an interference pattern can be illustrated by imagining that one drops three pebbles simultaneously into a shallow pan of water. The resultant waves will crisscross one another. If one were then to quick-freeze the surface ripples, one would have a record of the interference pattern made by the waves. When the interference pattern is then illuminated by a laser beam, the orange reappears as a three-dimensional image. This image is a hologram.[55]

An amazing characteristic of the holographic image is that the observer can change his or her perspective with respect to the image and perceive correspondingly different perspectives of the image as if he or she were looking at the original object. Also, if part of the photographic plate that contains the interference pattern is covered or removed, the image of the total object will still appear intact. Thus, it is said that each part of the interference pattern (analogous to a negative) contains information about the whole, hence, the name "hologram" from the Greek, *holos*, whole. One reason for the excitement that holography has caused in the neurosciences is that the behavior of holograms seems to provide a good model for the information-storing process of the brain. It was previously thought that information was stored in the brain in discreet areas, and if those areas were destroyed, the information would likewise be destroyed. One might refer to this as a computer model of the brain. But, in fact, the brain behaves more like a hologram than it does like a computer. Thus it is hypothesized that when the brain registers an item of information, or records an image, this information or record is diffused widely throughout the brain, and not contained in one locale.

How is holography different from conventional photography? Basically, conventional photography relies on the use of lenses and makes use of the refraction or reflection of light. Holography is based on a property of light that was described by Huygens and Grimaldi in the mid-1600s, called "diffraction." Diffraction is essentially a bending of wave energy around obstacles (e.g., the orange in Ring's example). Dia-

DIFFRACTION OF WAVES

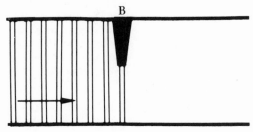

1 Water waves about to pass an obstacle extending into a channel.

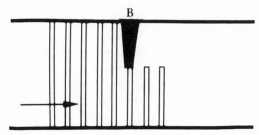

2 What *does not* happen when waves pass an obstacle.

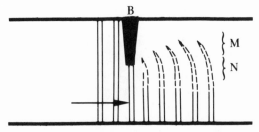

3 What *does* happen when waves pass an obstacle.

adapted from H. Klein, *Holography* (New York: Lippincott), 1970.

grams of how diffraction works are shown in Figures 1 through 3. Although the principle of diffraction has been known for some three hundred years,[56] it was not until the middle of this century that the first hologram was produced by Gabor. Gabor hoped to eliminate the distorting effect of lenses by developing a way to produce images without lenses. This required the use of a *coherent* light source, unlike that which we encounter in nature or in conventional photography. In explaining the principle of coherence, one could make an analogy to a choral group. If every member of the group decides to sing his or her own tune, we have incoherent sounds. In the same way, most light is made up of differing wave lengths, and in that sense, is incoherent. In order to capture the phenomenon of diffraction clearly, a source of coherent light is required. The laser beam provides just such a coherent source. My treatment of holography is admittedly sketchy, and I am largely ignorant of the finer points having to do with the physics of light and the photoemulsion processes involved. However, I do not believe it is necessary to be an expert on holography in order to understand one central point: holography is based on the known properties of light, and is readily understood in terms of contemporary physics. Although it may have a science-fiction flavor about it, the holographic phenomenon lies clearly within the bounds known physical reality. In order to produce a hologram, certain *physical* conditions must be met. In order to perceive a hologram, we make use of our *psychophysiological* apparatus (including the lenses of our eyes). It does not belong to another order of reality. It would appear, however, that Ring is invoking holography as a model by which to understand certain aspects of the near-death experience of the "disembodied consciousness." He states (and the emphases are his):

> I assume that the core experience *is* a type of mystical experience that ushers one into the holographic domain. In this *state of consciousness,* there is a *new order* of *reality* that one becomes sensitive to—a frequency domain—as time and space lose their conventional meaning. The act of dying, then, involves a gradual *shift* of consciousness from the ordi-

nary world of appearances to a holographic reality of pure frequencies. In this new reality, however, consciousness still functions holographically (without a brain, I must assume) to interpret these frequencies in object terms. Indeed, as Pribram himself has argued—and he is not alone in this—the universe itself seems to be organized holographically.[57]

Ring's statement certainly merits careful attention. Underlying it there appears to be an unstated philosophical assumption of monism. That is to say, there is a predisposition to believe that the universe consists of one ultimate reality, and that this reality is somehow holographic. While monism may be attractive, it is nonetheless a philosophical assumption, which has not been proven to the exclusion of dualism or pluralism. Admittedly, however, the dominant thrust of contemporary Western thought seems to be in the direction of the monistic position, and it has a great deal of momentum. And why shouldn't it? It seems that one is more likely to adopt a monistic view of the universe if one believes that there is one set of principles or body of knowledge that can explain everything. That makes for a nice, tidy universe with no loose ends. Certainly new phenomena will be discovered, but nothing *radically* different will emerge. That is very reassuring to some. In order for the intellectual momentum of monism to be changed, one must overcome the resistance of intellectual inertia (if I may borrow from physics a bit). It is this sense of reassurance that constitutes intellectual inertia.

I believe that Ring, in the tradition of post-Enlightenment science, is extending known physical principles (namely, those of holography) into a domain the nature of which might be physical, or might not be physical at all. From a strictly scientific stance, we simply don't know. Holography has provided an extremely useful model for understanding brain functioning, but in the near-death experience, we are no longer dealing with a brain. Ring, indeed, acknowledges that in the above quote. If the persons who went through near-death experiences *perceived* a reality of whatever kind (and they apparently perceived something, a very extraordinary something), by what mechanism (for lack of a better word) did they perceive and organize their experiences? His phrase "holographic reality of pure frequencies" (and in a later part of the same discussion, "We are presumably sensitive to a higher range of frequencies") leaves unexplained how a nonphysical entity can resonate to such frequencies. It appears to me that invoking a holographic explanation, while very intriguing, still begs the question.

At the end of his very interesting holographic interpretation of the near-death experience, Ring offers us his interpretation of the individual's experience of the awesome, loving light. A number of those who experienced the near-death phenomenon interpreted this being of light as "God," or some kind of divine presence. Ring prefers to consider their experiences as a coming into contact with one's "total self," or what in some traditions is called "the higher self."[58] He states that this experience is quite distinct from a projection. "The golden light is actually a reflection of one's own inherent divine nature and symbolizes the higher self."[59] In the subsequent paragraphs Ring makes his case for the higher-self hypothesis, without making at all clear exactly why it is preferable to a more dualistic interpretation of the near-death experience as an encounter with the Other. Indeed, at this point, I do not wish to take issue with this question. When encountering something as awesome as "God" we should of course expect that our language would begin to reveal its limitations. There is no compelling reason (to my way of thinking) why the God as Other and as within could not both be true at the same time. Later, I would like to venture my own interpretation of some aspects of the near-death experience. For the sake of argument at this point, however, I would like to stay with Ring's hypothesis of the higher self, to see where it may lead.

One place it leads is to the so-called "spiritual path," as Ring himself acknowledges:

> . . . readers familiar with various spiritual traditions will know that the point of many spiritual disciplines, such as meditation and prayer, is precisely to cultivate an awareness of one's higher self in order to align one's individual personality with it. It is believed that in this way one can live more

fully in accordance with the total being of which one's personality is but an expression.[60]

The implications of this view (which one might dub a "nonspecific spiritual" view of human nature) for personality theory in psychology and for psychotherapy are of great
significance. One can begin to see at this juncture the relevance of Needleman's quote, cited earlier, "The shrinks are
beginning to sound like gurus and the gurus are beginning to
sound like shrinks."[61]

If one accepts Ring's interpretation of the near-death experience as offering a glimpse of the so-called higher self, and
if one accepts this glimpse as providing a deeper (and in some
sense, truer) view of the dimensions of the human personality
than one encounters in contemporary personality theory and
psychotherapy (whether psychodynamic or humanistic), then
I think one should examine whether contemporary Western
psychotherapy leads its clients to align themselves more closely with their higher selves. I am, of course, making this suggestion for those who would accept Ring's nonspecific spiritual
view, but who would not accept a more Christian view that I
will offer later. At this point in the discussion, there really is
little difference between a nonspecific and a specific spiritual
view in terms of having implications for psychotherapy. I believe that most Christians would be quite comfortable with the
insights into human values and behavior offered by those who
have faced death.

The value changes are discussed at some length by Ring,[62]
but he does not make any connections between these value
changes and possible implications for psychotherapy. Chapter
eight of Ring's book discusses personality and value changes as
a result of the near-death experience. I believe that some of
the values that were heightened by the experience are directly opposed to some that have been fostered and exploited by
contemporary Western psychotherapy. One of the former values is the sense of duty or obligation. A good number of the
near-death survivors stated that one of the chief reasons for
returning to life was a sense of the duty to finish an unfinished

task. This, it seems to me, is a long way from the mentality fostered by the majority of contemporary therapists, wherin a sense of "duty" seems "oppressive," to use Lasch's terms.[63] Some of the survivors mentioned that they felt that God had a purpose for them, and they wanted to fulfill that purpose. Even if one is afraid of religious language (such as "God"), and prefers the more neutral "higher self," one can easily see that the measure of a full life can no longer be assumed to be that of the greatest pleasure.

A specific sense of duty or obligation is that in relation to loved ones. A good number of the survivors mention that they returned because their loved ones needed them. These survivors mention that "giving" has become much more important to them. Such altruism is seldom encountered in the parlance of contemporary psychotherapy. Indeed, it is often regarded as some kind of neurotic hang-up. Altruism has long been regarded as suspect by psychoanalysis, partly because some extreme cases of altruism can easily be understood as reaction formations (or sublimations), and partly because it is quite difficult to account for the survival of altruism from a natural selection point of view. On the first point, cases are easily cited by analysts of patients who were oversolicitous of people who they would unconsciously like to be rid of, and of cases where a solicitous or unselfish attitude was related to an unconscious sexual attraction. Because we have become used to looking for the hidden or "real" meaning of such behavior, we have tended to dismiss too much of altruistic behavior as having a selfish or sexual motive. Somehow, the hidden, or unconscious, motive for behavior has become equated with the real or true motive. While this approach, of not taking behavior at face value, was an enormous forward stride in understanding human behavior, I believe that it has been overused to the point of becoming somewhat arbitrary. There is no compelling reason why the unconscious motivation in a given situation should be any more "real" than a more conscious motivation.

In the present instance of the near-death experience, altruism suddenly increased in the survivors, apparently as a consequence of their encounter with another realm, or altered state of consciousness, if you prefer. In either case, this sudden increase of altruism presents a challenge for traditional psychology to interpret. I do not believe any of the traditional psychological modes of thought can offer a credible interpretation from within their own framework, whether it be psychodynamic, behavioristic, or existential-humanistic.

In like manner, those who have survived a near-death experience return with a change in their priorities with regard to the importance of material things. Ring reports that the survivors place less importance on material possessions.[64] From reading the protocols that Ring relates, one gets the impression that these people are more "detached" in relation to material possessions. How foreign is this attitude to twentieth-century America! Wherever did it come from? It certainly goes against years of operant reinforcement. The sense of duty, the desire to give to others, and the deemphasis on material possessions are certainly the antitheses of the values espoused by contemporary Western psychologies. Rather, they appear to reflect the ancient values espoused by a number of the world's great religions, what Needleman refers to as "the sacred tradition." If one grants that the near-death experience provides us with a glimpse of what it means to be fully human, and if the values derived from the experience add in any way to the depth of such humanity, it would seem reasonable (at least from a humanistic perspective) that such values might be fostered in psychotherapy. This is not to advocate a psychotherapy of religious indoctrination. We already have several psychotherapies that subtly communicate values, though quite unwittingly in most cases. What I suggest is that values be discussed more openly between therapist and client, and that therapists ought to explore whether incorporating some of the above values might be helpful to their clients. At the very least, the testimony of the near-death survivors should prompt therapists to examine their own system of values. It certainly provides a contrast to the value systems of the self-help industry, whose motto seems to be, "Look out for number one!" (Closely related to the "me first" mentality is the "my kids first" mentality, which is really just an extension of it. We frequently see books and articles of a "how to" nature designed to teach parents how to guarantee that their children will be "winners," which usually means that they will become very clever in exploiting their peers and winding up at the top of the heap.) Modern psychology has strengthened the notion that this is what life is all about. And where is it getting us?

Ring provides much evidence that his near-death survivors, as a result of their brush with death, exhibit a "heightened spiritual awareness."[65] He states:

> The increased religious feeling on the part of the core experiencers involved a sense of being closer to God, feeling more prayerful, taking less interest in formal religious services, but expressing greater tolerance for various forms of religious expression and endorsing an attitude of religious universalism.[66]

I believe that these people have experienced the universe as having values, and that their own value changes are a reflection of this.

At this point, I wish to introduce my own interpretation of the near-death experience, and its implications for psychology. In attempting to interpret the data of Ring, Moody, and others, I will also be borrowing from observations made in parapsychology to supplement the near-death data. Parapsychology is a field with a reputation for wild speculation, and indeed, that is a risk when dealing with intangibles. One criterion that I hope to use in sorting out the parapsychological data, and attempting to differentiate what is feasible from what is purely fanciful, is the "pragmatic truth test." Essentially, it involves borrowing from William James and from Bridgman's operationism to help decide what is real in the very confusing area of parapsychology. The "pragmatic truth test" assumes that if an operation (or behavior) works (i.e., accomplishes what was intended), it has "truth value"—that is, the hypothesis that prompted the operation is probably true. The hypothesis becomes even more persuasive if alternative hypotheses (which suggest different "operations") are tried and fail to accomplish the desired end.

Let me begin with an example from psychopathology to illustrate how the "pragmatic truth test" may be employed. Let us say there is a certain patient who is exhibiting a variety of psychiatric symptoms. Conventional psychotherapies and chemotherapies are employed. This "operation" is based on the hypothesis that the patient is suffering from one form or another of psychopathology included in the conventional psychiatric nosology. Let us assume, further, that this patient obtained no relief from traditional psychiatric treatment, and was referred, as a last resort, for LSD treatment. During the LSD treatment, the female patient's voice was transformed into that of a male, as were her facial features. In this "trance" or whatever, the patient displayed remarkable paranormal knowledge of people in the room. After trying to deal with these symptoms verbally, with no success, the psychiatrist then closes his eyes, meditates and visualizes all in the room surrounded by a white light ("operation #2"). He bases this on the hypothesis that the patient is possessed by a spirit, and he has read that evil entities don't like white light. Next, let us suppose that coincident with operation #2, the patient's symptoms disappear (even when she was unaware of the "operation" of the psychiatrist). This is an example of the "pragmatic truth test" as applied to a hypothetical case of pathological behavior, where the two competing hypotheses were those of: a) psychiatric disorder; b) possession by a spirit. In point of fact, the case is not hypothetical at all, but is fully documented by Stanislav Grof, M.D., who was the psychiatrist in question.[67] This and similar cases of possession by spirits are discussed by Ian Currie.[68] Currie cites another example of what I call "secular exorcism," wherein Dr. Walter Prince, a psychologist, treated a patient who was being harassed by the spirit of her dead cousin.[69] Similar cases would be classified as some form of schizophrenia, but Prince had noted that treating such cases "as if" they were schizophrenic was not successful. In the case of Mrs. Latimer, he treated her "as if" her cousin's spirit truly was harassing her. He dialogued with the "entity," explaining why it should depart and leave Mrs. Latimer alone. Result: it worked! The woman had no further symptoms from that session. To be purely pragmatic about these results, it appears that the hypothesis of "spirit possession" has more "truth value" than the alternative hypothesis of psychiatric abnormality.

Our cultural bias toward the assumption of psychiatric abnormality is illustrated by the case of the Yakima Indian girl treated by E. Mansell Pattison, M.D., of the Department of Psychiatry and Human Behavior at the University of California at Irvine.[70] While Pattison was in the U.S. Public Health Service, he encountered a young Yakima woman who began to display bizarre behavior, the onset of which was rather sudden, following an incident in which she and several of her friends claimed to have been pursued by spirits of their ancestors. The patient and her mother consulted with Dr. Pattison. The mother explained that in the "old days" such a problem would be handled by a tribal exorcism. However, since the Indian family were now good Presbyterians, that method might not be acceptable. As the girl had already been treated with chlorpromazine, apparently Pattison was open to suggestions. He indicated to the patient's mother that the tribal women should go ahead with the exorcism. Pattison reports that the girl was free of all symptoms from the time of the exorcism. In his concluding remarks, Pattison says of this case:

> This case illustrates the importance of the belief system—the cultural frame of reference—in the interpretation of behavior. The psychiatrist is limited in that he operates within a particular scientific world view of behavior. It is possible and appropriate to help others by enabling them to act within their own world view, even though it is fundamentally different from the psychiatric view.[71]

Once again, it appears that it is up to the tolerant white psychiatrist to make a concession to the superstitious aborigines, "to enable them to act within their own world view." I think Pattison missed the point of his experience. That is, by the criterion of the pragmatic truth test, "Who got results?" I rate the score in this case: Yakima women, one; chlorpromazine, zero. Perhaps it is they who should be reeducating us as to a more complete "worldview."

Let me offer one more example where the presumably unsophisticated approach scored a clear triumph over the sophisticated medical approach. The case is fully documented in the *Archives of Sexual Behavior.*[72] It involved a twenty-one-year-old transsexual with a "normal chromosomal pattern, without psychosis, defective judgment, or abnormal affect," who was fully prepared for sex-reassignment surgery. He had cross-dressed since the age of four. As a favor to a friend of his, on his way to the clinic to undergo surgery, he visited a physician of a fundamentalist Protestant background. After a thorough physical exam, the physician told him that his problem was "possession by evil spirits." After some discussion, a two- to three-hour exorcism was conducted by the physician. Immediately following this, the patient discarded his female clothing and announced that he was a man. After another session with a faith healer, the patient noticed that his breasts (whose growth had been accomplished by hormone therapy) suddenly disappeared. The patient's case was followed for two and a half years, and showed "a clear reversal of gender identity."[73] Hence, we have another case where exorcism succeeded in the treatment of a condition notoriously resistant to psychotherapy.

The point of relating the above cases is emphatically not to espouse that possession by spirits accounts for all psychopathology. The point is rather that by applying the pragmatic truth test evidence is enhanced that *there does exist a spirit world.* In all of the above cases, persons acted (or performed operations) in accordance with the hypothesis that they might be dealing with a spirit world rather than with some phenomenon having a purely materialistic explanation. In each case the spirit-hypothesis operation obtained results. It worked. That ought to be the chief (although admittedly not the only) criterion of veracity in scientific hypothesis formation and theory building. Instead, we often read of scientists fretting as to whether a phenomenon or its explanation fits into a worldview or not.

At this point I wish to return to the discussion of the near-death experience, and how I believe the foregoing studies shed some light on its interpretation. Ring hypothesizes that the survivors who report feeling the presence of God are, in his view, experiencing their higher selves. He does not say much about the spirits of deceased relatives and friends, and the religious figures that these people encounter. However, he refers to an experience of John Lilly, in which the latter experienced the presence of two spiritual guides while under the influence of LSD.[74] This is not unlike the meeting of spiritual entities experienced by the near-death survivors. In fact, Lilly says that these presences told him that they are always with him, but that he can perceive them only when he is close to his physical death. Ring seems to focus on the observation that these guides met by Lilly resembled guardian angels, and might have been a product of Lilly's early Catholic education.[75] However, Lilly himself states that it was during one of these LSD trips that he realized:

> I was to go through grief, through all sorts of emotions that I had been blocking off and refusing to recognize because of my "scientific knowledge." For the first time, I began to consider that God really existed in me and that there is a guiding intelligence in the universe.[76]

So who is to say which experience shaped (perhaps biased) Lilly's experience and his interpretation of it: his early Catholic education, or his later scientific training?

Another issue here is the use of language, which obviously shapes our interpretation of these accounts. As previously mentioned, language becomes inadequate when we begin to use it to describe unfamiliar domains of reality, particularly something as intangible as a spirit world. In testimony of this fact is the ancient Judaic wisdom that forbade pronouncing the name of God: Not only is it too sacred, but no mere human words could do it justice. In the instances described above, the near-death survivors and the exorcists all experienced the spirits as "other." Ring seems to prefer a view that these spirits are somehow manifestations of ourselves. I submit that his preference in this regard rests partly on a preference for a monistic view of the universe, which is, of course, quite widely held. Although language is an important factor in shaping one's perception of something as intangible as the "spirit world," the issue is of too great importance to be relegated to simply a semantic problem. To assert that the experiences of the near-death survivors bespeak a spirit world populated by "others," and not merely by ourselves, is of enormous consequence.

In the field of parapsychology, there are two chief competing hypotheses invoked to explain phenomena such as clairvoyance (which is exhibited in near-death experiences as well as exorcisms). They are the "survival hypothesis" (according to which the human personality is hypothesized to survive bodily death) and the "super-ESP hypothesis" (the view that a medium can telepathically locate distant persons and glean relevant information from them). In concluding his discussion on the possibility of discarnate survival, Gauld states:

> The continuity hypothesis and the super-ESP theory appear to have reached a position of virtual stalemate. Each can produce some sort of explanation of the other's most cherished data. The trouble is that the continuity hypothesis can give us no details of what it is that is supposed to survive, so that we do not know quite what to do to determine whether it is there or not. Likewise, the super-ESP theory is silent as to the laws and characteristics of ESP, so that we have no means of saying for certain whether or not it has been at work.[77]

Gauld's comments also reflect the fact that the super-ESP hypothesis is attractive because of the monistic attitude underlying it. Most of us have been conditioned to prefer viewing the universe as being made of one kind of stuff. We have gotten used to the idea that the visible world around us (including our own bodies) can be viewed as basically "all the same stuff." So the extension of this view to the hereafter and to paranormal knowledge phenomena (clairvoyance) is quite understandable. But that does not make it true. Besides, the mechanism invoked to preserve the monistic view, the so-called "super-ESP" hypothesis, does not "explain" anything as long as other ESP phenomena remain unexplained. In my view, the super-ESP hypothesis amounts to a *deus ex machina* (in more ways than one). It merely pushes a presumed solution to the problem into a more rarified realm. By making the explanation of these phenomena appear esoteric, the illusion is created that the explanation has, in fact, explained ESP. It has done nothing of the kind.

What, then, is the alternative? The alternative I choose is the "survivalist" hypothesis, with the further specification that what survives is more than the self alone in some kind of isolated existence. I believe the evidence points to a survival in relation to other survivors. Whether this kind of survival can be explained by our present mode of language, or our present concepts of physics, is (pardon another pun) immaterial. If this is dualism, then so it is. Once we have appreciated the reasonability of positing the existence of a spirit world, and seen that it is equally, if not more reasonable than any quasiscientific view thus far offered, it makes sense to ask, "How can we become acquainted with this spirit world?" The answer would appear to be: by examining the teachings of those who have had the most experience with such a world. I think psychologists must admit, at this point, that if they continue only within their own methodology to deal with the spirit realm, they are in over their heads. They must take what Needleman calls the "sacred tradition" seriously. This means looking at religious tradition not as simply an anthropological phenomenon made up of wishful thinking and superstition, but as containing great wisdom. This wisdom, to be sure, is sometimes mixed in with folklore, making it seem unsophisticated. It is the contention of this author that to disregard this ancient wisdom as foolish would itself be the height of foolishness. Where does one begin such a quest? There are many places where one could begin, but I have chosen a Christian perspective from which to make sense of the spiritual dimension of humanity. I invite the reader to examine this perspective with me in the next chapter, and to offer alternative perspectives as he or she may choose to do so.

Notes

1. Watson, J.B., *Behaviorism* (New York: People's Inst., 1924), pp. 3–4.

2. Delooz, P., "Who Believes in the Hereafter?" in *Death and Presence* (Brussels: *Lumen Vitae*, 1970).

3. Moody, R., *Life After Life* (New York: Bantam, 1975).

4. Ibid., pp. 182–183.

5. Grof, S. and Grof, C., *Beyond Death* (New York: Thames–Hudson, 1980), pp. 8–9.

6. Tillich, P., *The Shaking of the Foundations* (New York: Pelican, 1949).

7. Ring, K., *Life at Death* (New York: Coward, McCann & Geoghegan, 1980), pp. 219–220.

8. Siegel, R. K., "The Psychology of Life after Death," *American Psychologist*, vol. 35, (Oct. 1980), pp. 911–931.

9. Osis, K. and Haraldsson, E., *At the Hour of Death* (New York: Avon), 1977.

10. Rawlings, M., *Beyond Death's Door* (Nashville: Nelson), 1978.

11. Ring, op. cit.

12. Moody, *Life After Life*, pp. 21–23.

13. Ring, op. cit., p. 207 and p. 237.

14. Kübler-Ross, E., Interview on the *Tomorrow Show*, February 14, 1978, cited in Ring, op. cit., p. 207.

15. Bayless, R., *The Other Side of Death* (New Hyde Park, NY: University Books, 1971), cited by Ring, p. 207.

16. Hyslop, J.H., *Psychical Research and the Resurrection* (Boston: Small, Maynard & Co., 1908), cited in Ring, p. 207.

17. Moody, R., personal communication to Ring, cited in Ring, p. 239.

18. Rawlings, op. cit., p. 56.

19. Fiore, C. and Landsburg, A., *Death Encounters* (New York: Bantam, 1979), p. 123.

20. Lundahl, C., "The Near-death Experiences of Mormons," paper presented at the American Psychological Association convention, New York, August, 1979, p. 14.

21. Monroe, R.A. *Journeys Out of the Body* (New York: Doubleday, 1971).

22. Tart, C.T., "Out-of-the-Body Experiences," in Mitchell, E., ed., *Psychic Exploration* (New York: Putnam, 1974), pp. 349–373.

23. Ring, op. cit., pp. 74–76.

24. Moody, R., *Reflections on "Life After Life"* (New York: Bantam, 1977), p. 11.

25. Kübler-Ross, E., Interview on the *Tomorrow Show*, February 14, 1978, cited by Ring, p. 208.

26. Ring, op. cit., p. 208.

27. Lundahl, op. cit., pp. 10–12.

28. Ring, op. cit., pp. 211–212.

29. Noyes, R. & Kletti, R., "The Experience of Dying from Falls," *Omega*, vol. 3, 1972, p. 45.

30. Moody, R., *Life After Life*, pp. 164–166.

31. Moody, R., *Reflections on "Life After Life"*, pp. 109–110.

32. Ring, op. cit., pp. 206–217.

33. Moody, *Reflections on "Life After Life"*, pp. 24–27.

34. Ring, op. cit., pp. 218–252.

35. Hick, J.H., *Death and Eternal Life* (New York: Harper & Row, 1976), p. 12.

36. Ring, op. cit., p. 221.

37. Tart, C.T., "Out-of-the-Body Experiences."

38. Tart, C.T., "A Psychophysiological Study of Out-of-the-Body Experiences in a Selected Subject," *Journal of the American Society for Psychical Research*, vol. 62, no. 1, Jan. 1968, p. 21.

39. Tart, C., "A Second Psychophysiological Study of Out-of-the-Body Experiences in a Gifted Subject," *Parapsychology*, vol. 9, Dec. 1967.

40. Osis, K., "Out-of-the-Body Experiences: a Preliminary Survey," paper presented at the Parapsychology Association annual convention, St. Louis, August, 1978.

41. Tart, "A Psychophysiological Study of Out-of-the-Body Experiences," p. 21.

42. Osis, K., cited in Greenhouse, H.B., *The Astral Journey* (New York: Avon, 1974), pp. 280–290.

43. Ring, op. cit., pp. 218–252.

44. Moody, *Life After Life*, pp. 42–52.

45. Osis & Haraldsson, op. cit.

46. Rawlings, op. cit., p. 44.

47. Currie, I., *You Cannot Die* (New York: Methuen, 1978), pp. 94–98.

48. Ring, op. cit., pp. 224–232.

49. Morris, R., cited in Currie, op. cit., pp. 88–89.

50. Ring, op. cit., p. 233.

51. Rogo, D.S., *Parapsychology: A Century of Inquiry* (New York: Dell, 1975), p. 287.

52. Ibid., p. 287.

53. Ring, op. cit., pp. 218–252.

54. Pribram, K. "Holographic Memory," interview in *Psychology Today*, vol. 12 (Feb. 1979), p. 84.

55. Ring, op. cit., p. 235.

56. Klein, H.A., *Holography* (New York: Lippincott, 1970).

57. Ring, *loc. cit.*, p. 237.

58. Ibid., p. 240.

59. Ibid., pp. 240–241.

60. Ibid., p. 241.

61. Needleman, *A Sense of the Cosmos* (New York: Dutton, 1975), p. 110.

62. Ring, op. cit., pp. 138–158.

63. Lasch, C., *The Narcissistic Society* (New York: Norton, 1978), p. 13.

64. Ring, op. cit., pp. 143 ff.

65. Ibid., p. 185.

66. Ibid.

67. Grof, S., cited by Osis, K., in "Proceedings of the First Canadian Conference on Psychokinesis," *New Horizons*, vol. 1, no. 5, January 1975, p. 232; also cited by Currie, op. cit., p. 191.

68. Currie, op. cit., pp. 163–195.

69. Ibid., pp. 181–183.

70. Pattison, E.M., "Exorcism and Psychotherapy: A Case of Collaboration," in *Religious Systems and Psychotherapy*, R.H. Cox, ed. (Springfield, Illinois: C. Thomas, 1973), pp. 284–295.

71. Ibid., p. 294.

72. Barlow, D.H., Abel, G.G., and Blanchard, E.B., "Gender Identity Change in a Transsexual: An Exorcism," *Archives of Sexual Behavior*, vol. 6, no. 5, 1977, cited in Baars, C., *Feeling and Healing Your Emotions* (Plainfield, NJ: Logos International, 1979), pp. 205–206.

73. Ibid.

74. Lilly, J., *The Center of the Cyclone* (New York: Julian, 1972), pp. 37 ff.

75. Ring, op. cit., p. 244.

76. Lilly, op. cit., p. 91.

77. Gauld, A., "Discarnate Survival," in *Handbook of Parapsychology*, B. Wolman, ed. (New York: Van Nostrand Reinhold, 1977), pp. 615–616.

FIVE

Introducing
the Psychology of Jesus

A fresh look at the Christian doctrine of the soul can bring
us toward the cosmological element that is so lacking in
modern psychology, and by implication, in the way we think
about ourselves.

Jacob Needleman[1]

The researcher's narcissistically invested theory is perceived
to be perfect and capable of providing ultimate answers to
complex and seemingly unexplainable phenomena. In this
sense such a theory attenuates the scientist's sense of vulner-
ability and helplessness in the face of puzzling and inscruta-
ble data, which may shake the very foundation of one's
belief system.

Nowhere are irrational and narcissistic factors more likely to
impinge on the researcher's objectivity than in the investigation of what happens to us when we die. This is not a
dispassionate issue. Our beliefs about mortality and immortality shape the structure of our value systems and mold the
way in which we lead our lives. It comes as no surprise, then,
that many of the standards of interpretations of near-death
experiences are ultimately reductionistic because of this
need to make the data fit a pre-existing and narcissistically-
invested paradigm.

–G. Gabbard and S. Twemlow[2]

Even if the previous arguments concerning the nature of
the near-death experience are accepted, the question of
the meaning of the evidence is still unanswered. While Moody[3] and Ring[4] are quite careful to disavow their evidence as

constituting any kind of proof of the existence of an afterlife, Rawlings[5] finds the evidence quite convincing. The nearly universal bliss of these experiences is the cause of some skepticism among believing Christians. After all, if we are accountable for our behavior in this life, why do we so rarely hear of negative judgments of the life-review, or rarely hear of reports of a helllike realm? It is stretching the belief of most Christians a little too far to expect them to believe that God is some great nonjudgmental Therapist in the Sky. Moody has encountered exactly this kind of skepticism, when asked by one if his listeners if the whole phenomenon could be a trick of the devil.[6] His answer essentially is that those who survive the near-death experience generally continue their lives in a very constructive and ethical manner, which would presumably be at cross-purposes with those of the hypothetical demon. In other words, his interpretation is not unlike that of St. Paul, who indicated that the origin of supernatural events could be discerned by their fruits. However, the potential for being deceived in this realm should not be dismissed or underestimated. We might add here a very important observation by Rawlings, who, alone among the aforementioned authors, has had the opportunity to participate in the resuscitation efforts for the near-death survivors in his capacity as a physician. He states that on many occasions, the patient at the point of death would state that he or she had a "hellish" experience, but when questioned about it after recovery, perhaps just a few hours later, would adamantly deny that they had had any such experience.[7] Rawlings believes that a great many of those who remember nothing of their experience afterwards very likely had such negative experiences. When they are revived, the well-known phenomenon of repression could well come into play. However, there is another possibility. Rawlings himself underwent a near-death experience of a pleasant nature, but was forbidden to reveal certain things that he saw during it.[8] Could it be that other patients who have no trace of memory of their experience (assuming that they had such an experience) are constrained from remembering it by some supernatural means? There is obviously no clear answer to this question, as we are entering into a realm beyond our normal powers of knowing.

In the realm of what we might call the "transnatural," we are obviously on shaky ground because that realm seems to behave in ways that are sharply at variance with the ways in which the world of our ordinary senses behaves. Some will conjecture that we have left our everyday Newtonian universe (to which modern psychology seems to be irrevocably wedded) into a post-Einsteinian universe of curved space, time warps, quantum physics, holograms, *psi*, etc. All of this seems to me to be a last-ditch effort of the human intellect to contain the universe in a framework of materialistic monism. I believe that the near-death experience is but the threshold of a realm beyond that, and that there are other phenomena (such as documented cures and exorcisms) that simply defy monistic explanations, whether materialistic or neo-idealistic. It has been cited many times that Nietzsche declared that God was dead. It has been said that Sartre declared that science was dead. A good case could be made that it was only in the industrialized West that God was considered dead, and that even here, He is being reborn on a wide scale. Not very long ago, it was "in" to speak of the "post-Christian era." There are many who would agree that, indeed, in some sense, Christianity was dying, but many of these people would also agree that it is now undergoing a rebirth.

As mentioned, however, things are not always what they seem in the realm of the "transnatural." Modern people are used to relying on their sense of what is tangible, and we must give due credit to this empirical bent for getting us as far as it has from a technological point of view. When we leave that comfortable, sensible realm, however, all kinds of confusion sets in. We no longer have a clear sense of what is real. In the 1960s it was common for people to take hallucinogenic drugs to get in touch with their "real" selves. This mentality could even be regarded as an outgrowth of the previous generation's desire to get in touch with their "real" selves by being psychoanalysed, based on the unexamined assumption that somehow the unconscious was more "really me" than the conscious self. When the couch failed to lead to the ultimate answers (although one must admit, it did lead to a certain degree of self-knowledge), and pot became the opium of the younger set, some began to follow the folk hero Carlos Casteneda and his Don Juan, while those who were disillusioned with the drug scene and with therapy began to flock to the Maharishi and his Transcendental Meditation. Whether disillusioned by TM or disdaining the notion of vulgarizing meditation for the masses, others sought out Zen masters, went to ashrams in India, Tibet, or Philadelphia. One might add here the alternative routes of sensory deprivation, with or without LSD (as per John Lilly). It appears that these varied routes lead to encounters with what might be called "transnatural" phenomena. Among the transnatural phenomena frequently encountered is contact with what *appears* to be a spirit world.

The ultimate as far as the ability of the human mind to affect reality would appear to be found in various esoteric writings cited and discussed by Talbot. In *Mysticism and the New Physics,* he discusses the accounts of those who have practiced meditation that the "yoga master can create physical objects or *tulpas* by simply developing the powers of consciousness."[9] In some cases, these *tulpas* appear in the form of demons to test the meditator, whose task it is to resist believing in their reality, so as not to let the *tulpas* have power over him or her. Cases are cited by Talbot in which witnesses other than the meditator saw and felt these *tulpas,* and cases are cited in which practiced masters of meditation were found dead after an encounter with these *tulpas.* These "beings" appear to take on a life of their own, though Talbot says that one can only be defeated by them if one believes in them. Yet in his own discussion of them he refers to them as "physical objects." If Talbot isn't sure what they are, then I am certainly not either. However, my hypothesis is that they might well emerge from another realm of existence (call it the spirit world if you choose), and break into the physical world taking on whatever form they may. It is of more than academic interest to note that a very similar account is cited by Maloney in the context of Transcendental Meditation. He cites the experience of Vail

Hamilton, a former TM instructor. She meditated from three to ten hours a day (far more than the twenty minutes TM initiates are advised to do), and began to experience spiritual presences of a negative sort in her room:

> I had vivid experiences of demonic oppression while meditating intensely for three months. In the night, during sleep, I awoke with a sense of fear and apprehension as pressure was being put all over my head and body by a spirit who was trying to enter my body.[10]

Another popular meditating technique that promises great powers to those who pay for the complete course is Silva Mind Control. What is rarely mentioned in the Silva literature is that on the third night of the course, the initiate puts him- or herself the control of two spirit guides, called "counselors." At least two Silva students cited in Rath's article believe that the extrasensory powers achieved in Silva Mind control have their source in the spirit world, and are of the opinion that these spirits are not benevolent.[11] In other words, they are very possibly demonic. The parallel between the easy access to supernatural powers offered to would-be Silva students and the power of knowledge offered to Adam and Eve is striking. It would seem to demonstrate, once again, that there's no such thing as a free lunch.

It has become fashionable, even for those who are willing to accept the fact that altered states of consciousness are not achieved without risk, to assume that these "so-called" demonic manifestations are really the eruption into consciousness of content from a deep and archaic level of the unconscious. This kind of thinking is in keeping with the notion that the task of psychology is to study the contents of the psyche without attempting to make a statement as to the ontological or ontic reality of these contents. While that position may be intellectually safe and sophisticated, it is also very foolish. The fact is that science alone (whether it be psychology or physics) cannot demonstrate the reality or unreality of these "entities" and whether they exist apart from ourselves, but the basic question of their nature remains of enormous importance. I submit that the disciplines of psychology or meditation that shrug off this question are not sophisticated at all, but pseudosophisticated, and perhaps reckless.

Elmer Green speaks to this same issue, and states that the commercial mind control courses may be tapping into a realm of "low-grade" entities.[12] It is my own hypothesis that evidence for reincarnation might very well also derive from this realm, where information is transmitted and received seemingly from a previous existence. Of course, I am aware that my hypothesis may be shaped by my religious and philosophical frame of reference, and I do not pretend that it is proven. Nonetheless, I consider it a very reasonable hypothesis, if one accepts the survivalist framework.

It is at this juncture that my own Christian choice has an explicit influence in determining some of my positions. Frankly, if I am going to enter the so-called "astral plane," where it is possible to encounter almost anything, spiritual, material, or something that doesn't exactly fit either of these categories, I would like a guide who knows his way around, and who can be trusted. I could not, like Elmer Green, take the advice of a discarnate spiritual teacher who will not identify himself.[13] After all, one doesn't probe the depths of one's unconscious without knowing the identity of one's analyst. In the "astral realm," science (whether physics or psychology), is clearly inadequate to teach us what is real and what is not. There are many who are seeking guidance in these realms from Oriental religions. Something in me resists this, even though I once practiced Transcendental Meditation. Perhaps it is fear, prompting me to regress to my early Christian roots. Perhaps it is mistrust of the purveyors of Oriental religions. After all, the Maharishi Mahesh Yogi insists that TM is not a religion, in the face of very good evidence that it is a religion. I don't know if I would allow him to take me on a path that leads who knows where.

There is another reservation regarding the East that was put quite well by Jung:

> I saw that Indian spirituality contains as much of evil as of

good. The Christian strives for good and succumbs to evil; the Indian feels himself to be outside good and evil, and seeks to realize this state by meditation or yoga. My objection is that, given such an attitude, neither good nor evil takes on any real outline, and this produces a certain stasis. One does not really believe in evil, and one does not really believe in good. Good or evil are then regarded at most as *my* good or *my* evil, as whatever seems to me good or evil—which leaves us with the paradoxical statement that Indian spirituality lacks both evil and good. . . . [14]

Perhaps this is why some Oriental teachings appeal to modern psychotherapy; it is possible, through them, to utterly avoid taking a stance with regard to good and evil. I am convinced that the explanation for evil as being simply the absence of good (the *privatio boni* notion) is inadequate. It certainly is not adequate as a model of the human being in psychology. There is plainly such a thing as human maliciousness, which cannot be sufficiently explained as resulting from deprivation or trauma (although obviously these factors take their toll). In the end, people are not plants. The notion, therefore, that more and more manure will improve them is fallacious.

Returning to Eastern paths to enlightenment, I have another reservation. It strikes me that, in general, Oriental paths place too much exclusive emphasis on the intellect, to the neglect of active human concern for one's brothers and sisters. This seems to me quite removed from the Judaic emphasis on the *mitzvah,* or good deed. While "compassion" is listed as a component of enlightenment in Eastern writings, it seems to be of a very passive type. How often do we see it practiced, particularly toward the poor and needy? If Eastern religion practiced such compassion, what need would Calcutta have for Mother Theresa? Why are there no enlightened gurus helping her care for the human refuse of Asia's cities? Because the material world is just an illusion? Illusion or not, starvation and sickness hurt. If it be countered that even pain is an illusion, and that through enlightenment, one can be liberated from it, tell that to the homeless three-year-olds, crying in the streets. I believe it was Eldridge Cleaver who said, "If you're not part of the solution, you're part of the problem." Indeed, we are all part of the problem. The beginning of enlighten-ment is to realize it.

Many people in the West do not realize that all around them, at this very moment, lie records of the teachings of a person who knew his way very well in the astral sphere, and who not only taught compassion, but practiced it actively. His name was Jeshua, son of Joseph, better known as Jesus.

The evidence that Jesus "knew his way around the astral sphere" is very clear from the Gospels. This becomes espe-cially striking when one considers the context in which the Gospels were written. According to Hick, belief in the person-al survival of bodily death emerged in Hebrew thinking be-tween 800 and 200 B.C. whereas this concept existed in Egypt from the third millenium B.C.[15] Furthermore, the Hebrew notion of the afterlife was most often pictured as a kind of limbo *(sheol)*. "The general Old Testament view was that to go down to *sheol* was to pass forever out of the land of the living and out of the ongoing life of the nation in its covenant relationship with Yahweh."[16] At the time when Jesus was teaching, Jewish religious teachers were divided on the ques-tion of personal immortality: the Pharisees affirmed it, but the Sadducees denied it. Indeed, the Sadducees tried to catch Jesus in what they hoped would be a contradiction in his teach-ing on the afterlife (Luke 20:27–40).[17] Not only does Jesus affirm personal survival of death, but teaches the resurrection of the body, and suggests that it is in some respect different from our present earthly bodies. And he does this without the slightest hesitation or equivocation. How could a carpenter from Nazareth be so sure of such things?

Furthermore, Jesus' notion of the nature of the afterlife is clearly different from the more commonly held notion of *sheol*. As he hung on the cross, he promised the repentant thief, "today you will be with me in Paradise" (Luke 23:43). St. Paul continues the Christian notion when he uses the word "paradise" in describing what sounds like a near-death experi-ence (2 Cor. 12: 1–6). Incidentally, and probably in reference to this near-death experience, Paul asserts (not unlike Plato) that our ability to perceive and to know will be enhanced in the afterlife: "What we see now is like a dim image in a mirror; then we shall see face to face" (1 Cor. 13:12).

Other early Christian concepts of the afterlife appear to have some parallels with scenes described by experiencers of the near-death phenomenon. St. John's vision from Revelation (20–21) is recounted by Hick as follows:

> We are told that on this new earth, there is no more death; there is perpetual day with no night; and the holy city is described in poetic language as being made of precious metals and stones symbolizing inconceivable beauty and worth. Thus the new universe is not, like this one, a process of temporal change—birth, death, growth and decay—and the new earth is not a planet circling the sun. Such a state of affairs is not *this* world transformed, but a new and different environment altogether. It is a "new earth" only in the sense that it is a new situation, a different environment, another "world." This new world is not composed of the same matter as our present earth. . . . What the writer is saying is that redeemed and perfected human beings will find themselves in an ultimate situation in which God will be known as an all-pervasive presence.[18]

That personal survival of death is eternal is quite certain in Jesus' teachings. It is alluded to no less than five times in the sixth chapter of St. John's Gospel alone.

It was the belief of the early Christians, and remains the teaching of most Christian churches today, that the Resurrection of Jesus prefigured the resurrection of the bodies of all people, (Nicene Creed, A.D. 325). The Acts of the Apostles states, "There will be a resurrection of the just and the unjust." (Acts 24:15) If Jesus' Resurrection was to prefigure in some way the resurrections of other human beings, then one could conclude that there might be some (unspecified) similarities between Jesus' resurrected body and ours. Early Christian writings recognized the special attributes of Jesus' resurrected body. About a dozen accounts are given in the New Testament. The resurrected body seems to have had unearthly properties, suddenly appearing and disappearing, passing through locked doors, etc. But it also had physical properties, such as breaking bread, eating food, and being physically touched by a doubting Thomas. Sometimes Jesus' resurrected body was seen only by a select few, but on at least one occasion, by a large number (1 Cor. 15:6). The Gospel writers seem to have been well aware of the "special nature" of the resurrected body, but do not try to explain it. Indeed, how could one explain it? Looking back from the twentieth century, however, it seems that the "unearthly" characteristics of Jesus' resurrected body have some parallels with characteristics of the so-called "double" described by Ring and the various authors he cites.[19] What is strikingly different, however, is that Jesus' resurrected body also had a kind of physical reality that was lacking in the "doubles." There seems to have been something therefore unique in the Resurrection of Jesus, something clearly beyond the known categories of human thought. There are many who would dismiss the whole account of the Resurrection as a series of hallucinations and/or fabrications. However, there are increasing numbers of people (knowledgeable and scientific people) who are taking a second look, in the light of the truly inexplicable phenomenon of the Shroud of Turin.[20] Any attempt to dismiss the veracity of the Resurrection story must explain how the Shroud came to be.

Many intellectual people find the account of the Resurrection a serious stumbling block, which prevents them from examining Christianity further. But it is precisely because the Resurrection is unfathomable by means of the intellect that it is important. One of Jesus' central messages was that the intellect should be subordinate to love. While the intellect is certainly to be esteemed, it is not the highest faculty of human beings, and we ought to recognize its limits. This is certainly Paul's understanding of Jesus' message when he discusses love in 1 Corinthians 13: "I may have all knowledge and understand all secrets . . . but if I have no love, this does me no good."

It is also in Paul that we have one of the clearest descriptions of the resurrected human body:

> This is how it will be when the dead are raised to life. When the body is buried, it is mortal; when raised, it will be immortal. When buried, it is ugly and weak; when raised, it will be

beautiful and strong. When buried it is a physical body; when raised, it will be a spiritual body (1 Cor. 15: 42–44).

Although Paul appears to be describing here the resurrection on the last day, there are parallels between his description and those of people who have had near-death experiences. Rawlings has also pointed this out.[21] Before one can develop a psychology of the total human being, one should ask what that psychology conceives the human being to be. It appears to me that early Christianity had a very highly developed sense of the human as both physical and nonphysical. As Westerners entered the Enlightenment of the eighteenth century and continued into the early twentieth century, the nonphysical aspect was downplayed, or denied, by many. Only in the last third of the twentieth century is it beginning to appear that this "Christian metaphysics" of the human being may be more accurate than so-called scientific descriptions. Psychology, having been born in the nineteenth century, seems to be having some difficulties with this.

It is largely because the realm of metaphysics is beyond our senses, and therefore beyond empiricism, that it has been so deeply mistrusted by modern people. It seems, on that account, to have been dismissed and/or avoided. But doing that won't make metaphysical issues go away. They keep coming back to haunt us, as it were. The metaphysical dimension of human beings can no longer be ignored by any modern psychology that espouses to be a complete and nontruncated psychology. If one preaches, teaches and does therapy to "live life to the fullest," it is important to consider what life consists of. The objection that such questions lie beyond psychology is only an indictment of psychology. The question of what life consists of is still important, psychology's limitations notwithstanding. Psychology deals with human behavior, and the meaning of that human behavior is vastly altered depending on how one sees it fitting in to the "Big Picture." Values suddenly take on an added importance. Chapter two was devoted to showing how psychology is already involved in affecting values, whether it wants to or not.

It is of more than passing interest to note that the sense of detachment from earthly possessions experienced by those who were resuscitated was also central to the message of Jesus. Jesus bids those who would follow Him to "sell all you have and give the money to the poor, and you will have riches in heaven; then come and follow me" (Luke 18:22). The message to detach oneself from worldly goods is repeated by Jesus: "How hard it is for rich people to enter the Kingdom of God! It is much harder for a rich person to enter the Kingdom of God than for a camel to go through the eye of a needle" (Luke 18: 24–25). And again, Jesus says, "You cannot serve both God and money" (Matt. 6: 24). The message to "detach" has been repeated down the centuries by Christian mystics, as for example, in the Spiritual Exercises of St. Ignatius Loyola. Independently of the Christian tradition, Ian Currie gives accounts of discarnate entities that appear to be stuck to their earthly attachments, and unable to enter the realm of light described by those who have experienced death.[22]

How different this is attitude from the "me first" mentality! Apart from the question of whether utilitarian and hedonistic approaches to life are appropriate or moral is the question of whether there is not a more truly liberating way to be. If one could truly say, "It really doesn't matter whether I have more material things than X," what a burden would be let go! All that anxiety about competition with others, about wanting to get every last ounce of enjoyment from material things, would be diminished. How often do we, as therapists, deal with the feelings of inferiority of people who see themselves as only as valuable as their paychecks, or even those who bring home big paychecks and are beginning to resent the fact that others value them primarily because of their money-earning ability? Along with money, one could mention power, beauty, intelligence, physical prowess, etc. What good is any of it, unless it is subordinated to something greater? Sometimes those who possess some of the foregoing traits more than others seem to think they created all their own attributes, which in turn have brought them wealth, power, etc. Followed to the extreme, the Horatio Alger myth of "I made it all by myself, and it's all mine" certainly causes no end of social and psychic disruption. Viewed from a Christian perspective, the basic premise is also mistaken.

The belief that we have created our own strengths leads to an overpossessiveness toward them, to an aggrandizement of the self, and often to a disdainful attitude toward those less fortunate than we. Conversely, if we feel that we have less than others, we may soon come to believe that we *are* less than they. The realization that we are not our own creations, but partake of gifts that go beyond what even our families could give us, and which flow ultimately from the Creator is emphasized in both the Old and New Testaments. This realization, then, can become the basis for a path of liberation that is a way of asceticism. To the average person, asceticism (or one might say "detachment") has been associated with the dreaded "puritanism," which, in turn, has been associated with all kinds of repression. The equating of asceticism with puritanism is erroneous, as Needleman points out:

> As in other traditional teachings, Christian asceticism was in part a struggle to break down man's psychological dependence on the accidents of external bodily sensations. Between this understanding and what we now call "puritanism" there obviously lies a wide gap. The true ascetic struggles against the power of his false self, the ego, which is formed out of a distorted attraction to pleasure and an excessive fear of its absence. According to Evelyn Underhill's sensitive and reliable study of medieval Christian mysticism, the aim of bodily asceticism was the death (mortification) not of the body, but of selfhood (the ego) in its narrow individualistic sense.[23]

If there were no hope of a liberation from life's trials, then the path of detachment, or the death of the narrow self, would be crazy, or at least masochistic. And that is pretty much the message of modern psychology. How often one hears the modern therapeutic community deride efforts to free the higher self by curbing the narrow or lower self as sick. If one accepts a materialistic metaphysics without question, of course it *is* sick, maybe even schizophrenic. But that is precisely why a different metaphysics is worth exploring. By reacting so strongly to the weaknesses of contemporary religion, Needleman says that science—especially psychology—is guilty of a reaction that assumes that there is no help for us "out there."

> In moving to that extreme, in denying the existence of higher levels of intelligence in the external universe, it never finds its way to search for these same levels within man himself, levels of receptivity, organs of intelligence which can mirror in microcosm the laws of a conscious universe. It seems to me that the error of humanism—the error of modern psychology—is not that it seeks for help within man alone, but that it radically underestimates just what it is that can be found within man. But to glimpse such high possibilities in man it is necessary to have a system of cosmology, a metaphysics that communicates the existence in reality of these levels.[24]

What is it then, that Christianity finds within the human being? When his listeners asked Jesus whence would come the Kingdom of God, he replied, "The Kingdom of God is within you." Was he referring to something similar to what Needleman alluded to in his phrase "levels within man himself, levels of receptivity, organs of intelligence which can mirror in microcosm the laws of a conscious universe"? Or was he saying perhaps that and more? His listeners, of course, were expecting Jesus to speak of an earthly, material kingdom. But he surprised them by speaking of a spiritual Kingdom. And so it is with modern people, seeking salvation in self-help books, learning to amass more and more, and enjoying it less and less. Perhaps this is so because buried deeply under all the "look-out-for-number-one" dross is a faint, unconscious sense that there must be more to it than all this.

It seems to me that one of the central thrusts of Jesus' message, and one which has much relevance to modern psychology, is his repeated attack on the ego and its conceit that it can master everything. Freud, of course, pointed out quite correctly that the ego is not master of its own house, but psychoanalysis and the schools of thought that trace their origins to it, nevertheless held that the intellect would ultimately rule

supreme and make the irrational subject to the rational—
"Where id was, there ego shall be." One could argue that it
was a corruption of Freud's thinking that has led to the widespread expectation that reason holds the key to the mysterious
secrets of the psyche. Nonetheless, the analysts and other therapists were and are widely believed to "know" something the
rest of us don't: the meaning of our dreams, the meaning of our
behavior. And there is something almost esoteric in this intellectual exercise. A select group are believed to be privy to
these secrets, while the unwashed masses remain ignorant. To
some extent, this style also typifies the manner in which Eastern paths have been introduced into the West. (I do not presume to comment on the manner in which the Eastern paths
are experienced or introduced to those who are indigenous to
those cultures. However, I suspect that a similar critique could
be made of that as well.) To illustrate my point, let us consider
again the case of Transcendental Meditation. TM has been
mass-marketed in the United States for a number of years
now, and its popularity is evidence of some kind of hunger in
us and in our society. The initiation rite, however, consists of
the imparting by the instructor to the initiate of the mantra,
the meaning of which is not given to the initiate. Not only that,
the initiate is forbidden to reveal his or her mantra to anyone
else. One sometimes hears TM initiates teasing one another
with, "I'll tell you my mantra if you'll tell me yours." Most are
afraid to tell, perhaps because of a fear that its magical power
will somehow be lost. When asked how many mantras there
are, since each initiate is given a personal mantra, I have heard
instructors say, "More than one, but not an infinite number."
There is something very undemocratic about all this secrecy.
We have an "in" group and an "inner" group. It seems to me
somehow like an elaborate intellectual game. When one at-
tends a meeting of some of the various esoteric groups, the air
is heavily intellectual.

What is refreshing in the Judeo-Christian tradition is that it
is more democratic. One doesn't have to be intellectual to
follow Jesus. It is significant that from the thousands of verses
in the Old Testament, Paul chooses a quote from the prophet

Isaiah (29:14) to set the tone for the role the intellect is seen to play in following the Christian path:

> I will destroy the wisdom of the wise and set aside the understanding of the scholars. (Isaiah 29:14) So then, where does that leave the wise? or the scholars? or the skillful debaters of this world? God has shown that this world's wisdom is foolishness. (1 Corinthians 1:2)

This is not to say, however, that Christianity did not have a solid intellectual base from the beginning. When Jesus was twelve years old, he was found in the Temple, "sitting with the Jewish teachers, listening to them and asking them questions. All who heard him were amazed at his intelligent answers" (Luke 2: 46–47). Later in his life, Jesus was challenged by the worldly-wise Sadducees, the "eggheads" of the day, and he confounded them with his answers. But Jesus spent a greater part of his time bringing his message to the poor and illiterate, the unwashed masses. Some regarded these people as less valuable because they were not conversant with, or perhaps did not keep, all the intricate nuances of Mosaic Law. The special status of the poor is central in the message of Jesus, and it is one of the great scandals of those who call themselves "Christian" that they have so often disregarded and oppressed the poor, and continue to do so. If we can free ourselves from the corruptions in Christianity that have accumulated down through the centuries, and examine Jesus' message regarding the poor, it is possible to see that his attitude toward the poor is closely linked to his message of liberation from the narrow self. The poor will be better able to enter the Kingdom of Heaven than the rich (Matthew 19:23).

Equally radical is a quote found in Luke's Gospel:

> Watch out and guard yourselves from every kind of greed because a person's true life is not made up of the things he owns, no matter how rich he may be. (Luke 12:15)

In the modern idiom, one might say that Jesus was engaged in consciousness-raising of the poor as well as of the rich. The more conscious we become of the transitory nature of our possessions, the freer we become of them, and the better able to love.

One could also make the case that possessiveness also gives rise to the false belief that we have created our own abilities. We are urged to make good use of the abilities we have, and the effort to do so is a virtue, but it is a serious error of pride to believe that the raw material from which our talents developed is of our own making. If one may call this realization the beginning of "enlightenment," it could be said that such an enlightened view could only have a salutary effect on interpersonal relationships. How often does false pride, breeding jealousy, poison human relationships! If narcissism is the disease of our age, the message of Jesus may provide just the right corrective. The world is sorely in need of humility.

> The greatest in the Kingdom of Heaven is the one who humbles himself and becomes like this child. And whoever welcomes in my name one such child as this, welcomes Me. (Matthew 18:14)

Mother Theresa sees in the faces of every unwanted child, of every downtrodden derelict, the face of Jesus himself. It is that enlightenment that enables her to love. Who would the followers of Krishnamurti see, and how would they respond? The Hare Krishna disciples would not act to help such people, for fear of interfering with their karma.[25] While followers of Jesus have been ridiculed as being too "other-worldly," you really can't be more down-to-earth than Mother Theresa.

This may begin to sound like social philosophy rather than psychology. Whatever the case, the two are necessarily interwoven in the fabric of human experience. This, at least, would seem to be one of the tenets of the recently developing field of "community psychology," where the mental health of the individual is seen to be to a very great extent related to the type of community in which he or she lives. It is the fond hope of many that the insights offered from the perspective of "community psychology" will go a long way in revolutionizing and improving mental health systems. What is crucial, however, to the realization of this hope is the concept of "community." Often we hear the expression "a sense of community." It is perhaps a nebulous and complex concept, but I would hazard to say that the expression conveys something like "good feeling" or a "friendly atmosphere" that permeates a given group of people living in proximity to each other. No "community" can exist unless there is developed a high degree of empathy for one's fellow human beings. Until our society adopts a philosophy that gives more than lip service to the value of each person, it seems doubtful that a "sense of community" can be established. Seeing persons as beings who will live forever makes it difficult ever again to reduce them to statistics that fall into this or that category. It seems to me highly doubtful that a narrowly materialistic society, whether capitalist or socialist, can ever develop a deep sense of community. In order to arrive at a sense of community, we will have to begin taking seriously the command to love our neighbor. Nowadays such notions strike many people as corny or old-fashioned. But they just might be necessary for our survival.

The call to love one's neighbor as oneself was derided by Freud in *Civilization and its Discontents* as "impossible."[26] Yet, three years later (1934), as pointed out by Hans Küng, we find the same Freud, in a letter to Albert Einstein, calling for "love without sexual aim," as an indirect way of opposing war:

> There is no need for psychoanalysis to be ashamed to speak of love in this connection, for religion itself uses the same words, "Thou shalt love they neighbor as thyself."[27]

Küng believes that Freud himself practiced love of neighbor, but couldn't admit it in theory.[28]

For Freud to say that the ideal set forth by Jesus was impossible to attain, however, may have been very much to the point. The point that Freud seems to have missed (and which I also did not see) is that the very difficulty in loving everyone, even one's enemies, confronts us with our own egotism. Jesus appears not only to have been teaching an ethics of human conduct, but at the same time, confronting us with the narrowness of our own selves. The invitation to love our enemies can be viewed as wildly unrealistic, or as a challenge to enter into a growth process that is continually ongoing. It is only if we view it in the latter way that we can realize the difficulty of the challenge, even while we accept it, and become humble. Somehow, being humble is also being more realistic, because the reality is that we are all unfinished, self-involved beings, who did not create the raw material of ourselves. But this is a hard truth to confront. It is easier be complacent about ourselves, and to imagine that we are the center of everything. To me that seems more like fantasy. Jesus, on the other hand, is continually assaulting the complacent ego, and telling us that we have a long way to go. That is the path he blazes for us. It is a path of countless little deaths to the self that enrich the self and make it more alive.

The complacent, of course, include far too many who call themselves "Christians." They seem to think that having a salvation experience is the end of the path. It is only the beginning. The path is never completely finished in this life, and perhaps not in the next either. As Abbé Huvelin wrote, *"Je n'aimerai jamais assez."* ("I shall never love enough.")[29] It is the realization, the dawning in consciousness if you will, that one will "never love enough," because there are so many people in need of love, that should shake up the complacency of Christians, and especially cause them to rethink their relationship to the poor as a relationship to Christ himself. Such a realization might result in a new awareness of "community." Community psychology could thus benefit from a Christian input. Jesus' words, "You will always have the poor with you" (Matthew 26:11; Mark 14:7; John 12:8) have been used by some Christians as a justification for not helping the poor in need. Such an interpretation has to be one of the most twisted possible. If we are to love our enemies, we can hardly ignore the poor. On the contrary, "You will always have the poor with you" is a realistic appraisal of the human condition in an imperfect world. It can also be viewed as an invitation to give of the self to find oneself. In an imperfect world, there will always be some who don't seem to have their share of wealth, or health, or love. There will never be a lack of opportunity to enrich the lives of others, whether materially, emotionally, or spiritually.

While the foregoing view of the human dilemma may seem to some as too "religious" to be taken seriously by modern psychology, the following quote demonstrates that these concerns are shared by at least one prominent psychologist whose writing is definitely secular in nature:

> If there is a devil, it is not through sin that he opposes God. The devil's strategy for our times is to trivialize human existence in a number of ways: by isolating us from one another while creating the delusion that the reasons are time pressures, work demands, or anxieties created by economic uncertainty; by fostering narcissism and the fierce competition to be number one; by showing us the personal gains to be enjoyed from harboring prejudices and the losses from not moving out whenever the current situation is uncomfortable; fostering in us the illusion of self-reliance, that sly devil makes us mock the need for social responsibility and lets us forget how to go about being our brother's keeper—even if we were to want to.[30]

I am substantially in agreement with Zimbardo's analysis of contemporary society. If other secular-minded persons are also in agreement with him, I would invite them to consider the ego-jolting psychology of Jesus as a possible remedy for some of the aforementioned ills.

Let us return to the directive to love our enemies, probably one of the most difficult stumbling blocks on the Christian path. It puts us squarely in the realm of human conflict, which occupies a considerable percent of the time spent by psychotherapists with their clients. The admonition to do good for one's enemies actually predates Jesus' life on earth, and can be traced back into the Jewish scriptures:

> If your enemy is hungry, feed him; if he is thirsty, give him a drink; for by doing this you will make him burn with shame. (Proverbs 25: 21–22)

In the Old Testament, there seems to be a clear recognition of the natural human desire to feel superior: in this case, morally superior. The incentive to do good for the enemy is to derive satisfaction by embarrassing him or her. While this recommendation to do good for the enemy just to show him or her up might result in a change of heart in the enemy, and a lessening of conflict, the motives for loving one's enemy that Jesus espouses are different:

> Love your enemies and do good to them; lend and expect nothing back. You will then have a great reward, and you will be sons of the Most High God. For He is good to the ungrateful and the wicked. Be merciful just as your Father is merciful (Luke 6: 35–36).

The admonition to love one's enemies does appear to go against the grain of human nature. The natural tendency for most of us is to get back at someone who has hurt us or intends to hurt us. Some people view the notion of loving one's enemies as a form of masochism, and therefore somehow not mentally sound. But this is a superficial view. Frankl observed that those prisoners in concentration camps who had meaning in their lives were more likely to endure the abominations of the camps and to survive.[31] It is when loving the enemy is viewed from a different perspective that it becomes more meaningful, and therefore, more possible.

Some Christians have followed the admonition to love their enemies so well that they have tended to deny that they are even angry with them. Modern psychology, chiefly those forms of psychology traceable to Freud, have correctly pointed out that denial of anger is not good for us. It can lead to high blood pressure, headaches, and other psychosomatic symptoms. Also, if anger is not recognized and accepted as part of us, it can be displaced onto some innocent victim, or projected (that is, seen to be coming from someone else rather than from within ourselves).

So how are we to deal with our anger at those who hurt us? One suggestion from modern psychology has been to ventilate it onto an inanimate object. Classified ads list places where you can write away for foam rubber bats to hit against some object that stands for the enemy. Some suggest punching a pillow or an inflated clown to work off anger and hostility. Others sug-

gest a vigorous sport to work it off. Still others suggest assertiveness training, teaching the person how to express anger in
a constructive way, not allowing it to build up. There is also
the rational-emotive approach, where the aim is to reinterpret
the anger-provoking situation, thereby neutralizing some of
the anger. Displacing anger onto an inanimate object does not
seem to work for all people. Assertiveness training has certainly helped some of the "doormats of the world" develop health-
ier ways of coping with interpersonal conflicts. If these
methods work for some people, and no one is harmed by them,
I can see no objection to them. Likewise with the reinterpretative approach. In the reinterpretative (or rational-emotive)
approach, we may find some elements that could be said to
dovetail with the Christian approach to anger. An example
might be that a close friend steals money from us. We naturally get angry. Later we find out that this person has a drug
habit, and did not act out of malice but out of desperation. Our
feelings of anger toward him or her would probably diminish.
Through our understanding of human nature, largely derived
from modern psychology, we can be in a better position to
forgive because we understand, and yet still set standards of
behavior, so that some behaviors are regarded as unacceptable, even though "understandable."

Although the "reinterpreting" method of dealing with
anger can be integrated with the Christian ideal of loving
one's enemy, there is still something radically different about
Jesus' admonition to love our enemies and forgive those who
hurt us. That radical difference is the healing that comes with
forgiveness. It is a type of healing (or therapy) that again challenges the one who seeks healing, and again jolts the ego.
Anger is seen as a burden, which, if nurtured, can become
poisonous, and even contagious. As long as we nurture it, we
are unable to love, and a thousand opportunities to love pass
us by. Not only is it difficult to love our "enemies," but it is
difficult to love those whose love we want but are denied:
those whom we love but who let us down by not returning our
love. They, in a sense, become our "enemies" at that point.
This kind of difficulty in interpersonal relationships is more

often presented by the client in psychotherapy than a conflict over loving one's supposed "enemies" (be they the Communists, or another ethnic or racial group).

Kelsey gives a good example of this when describing a girl who found it quite easy to visit a sick friend in the hospital, day after day, for weeks. She was then asked how she would react if she were to get sick, and the same friend made no effort to visit her. She was immediately confronted with how her own unconscious expectations could lead easily to resentment if her friend did not reciprocate her concern.[32] Probably all of us face this kind of problem at some time in our lives. How often do we see this kind of inequality in the need for love, or inequality in the giving of love, lead to resentment. Some of us are strong enough to shrug off this kind of lack of reciprocity; others are not so fortunate. The rational-emotive therapy approach would point out that the girl cited by Kelsey was hanging on to an illogical and erroneous assumption, "If I show concern for X, then X must show equal concern for me." Those who are involved in assertiveness training would probably counsel this girl to tell her friend how his behavior makes her feel. Neither of these views seems to me to be incompatible with a Christian psychology. However, it would appear that Jesus would ask this girl to reflect on her resentment as stemming from unconscious egotism and perhaps as evidence of unnecessary worldly attachment. Christian healing would try to help this girl forgive in order to heal the hurt and anger.

Forgiveness is central in Jesus' message. The fact is that we all seek love, and our feeling or hope is that it will be returned when given. People who are among the have-nots as far as receiving love are naturally at a disadvantage in this world. While psychotherapy might help such people discover why it is that they find themselves in such a situation, they might not be in a position to change the situation. If one were to keep a "love ledger," they would remain in the red. It is at this point that the Christian religious experience, that is, the experience of Jesus, enters.

At this point I suspect that many readers will object that we are no longer in the domain of psychology, but clearly in that of "religion." We have left "reason" and are in the realm of "faith." Maybe. A psychology that flatly refuses to consider continued personal existence in the afterlife makes such an assertion on "faith" also. More precisely, it *chooses* to disregard some very compelling evidence for survival (as presented in chapter four). Such a psychology is unable to bolster the love-deficient person with a sense of self-worth. On the other hand, if you're eternal, you've got to be worth something! Furthermore, if life does go on, then the message of Jesus may not be illusory after all. In meeting rejection, one may confront one's own ego, and in dying to it, grow in depth and strength. Liberation from the self is tough, but the reward is great.

Insights from modern psychology have taught us that anger (such as that discussed above) is frequently caused by some unconscious fear. A very common fear is that of being rejected. It is when the individual can be helped to see how his or her anger is intensified by this fear that he or she can get a handle on the anger, so that it does not become all-pervasive. It is the Christian view that fear is conquered by love: There is no fear in love; perfect love drives out all fear (1 John 4:18). Often rejection can trigger considerable anger because it relates in some way to a fear that may have been experienced much earlier in life. Many secular psychotherapists would probably agree with this. Where a Christian psychology would differ would be in emphasizing that love is central in a radical way. It is central to all emotional growth and well-being; intellectual activity should be subordinate to love ("Woe to knowledge that does not lead to love," said St. Augustine), and finally, love is the central cosmological reality. This last point seems to have been shared by Jung in the latter part of his career, when he wrote:

> For we are in the deepest sense the victims and instruments of cosmogonic "love." I put the word in quotation marks to indicate that I do not use it in its connotations of desiring, preferring, favoring, wishing and similar feelings, but as something superior to the individual, a unified and undivided whole. Being a part, man cannot grasp the whole.[33]

In more human terms, Jesus said to his disciples, "My commandment is this: Love one another as I have loved you" (John 15:12). If these words were put into practice, what a boost community mental health would have! Much fear and much anger would be diminished. Loving one another, of course, is not limited to Christians. Indeed, the great scandal of Christianity has been the lack of love too often shown by Christians. Christian hypocrisy in this area is sometimes ridiculed by those who point to the "Kill a Commie for Christ" mentality. If we return to the message of Jesus himself and that of his disciples, we see that love becomes the basis not only for a psychology, but an ethics and a metaphysics as well.

There is already an ample and growing literature on Christian healing in relation to psychotherapy.[34] Most of this literature is based on the works of the early disciples of Jesus, who received the Holy Spirit as he had promised them. They then became channels of healing, healing of physical, emotional, and spiritual infirmities, by invoking the name of Jesus, as he had instructed them to do. Christians today are continuing this activity, in spite of criticism from fellow Christians, as well as from nonbelievers. That they should continue this work is fitting for, as Kelsey points out, fully one-fifth of all the Gospel passages relate to healing. That Jesus did heal a variety of real infirmities (not merely hysterical illnesses) seems uncontestable:

> In the *Talmud* (Sanhedrin 43a) we find the tradition that Jesus of Nazareth was hanged on a tree on the Passover Eve because he practiced sorcery; he was destroyed because he healed by calling upon evil forces rather than upon God .... Even his opponents did not try to contest the fact that Jesus healed but only to cast doubts upon the agency through which he did it.[35]

Because the literature on Christian healing is quite well developed, it would be redundant to expound on it further. For the reader who is interested, there are many sources by which to pursue it. The purpose of this book is to provide a bridge between secular psychology (which I feel is inadequate in many areas) and a Christian psychology, which might otherwise have appeared totally unfeasible to the secular reader. The literature on Christian healing of emotional and interpersonal problems ("inner healing") often makes use of insights developed by modern psychology. It is my view that a Christian psychology has much to learn from secular psychology, and that secular psychology has much to learn from the teachings of Jesus. It is my hope that all such knowledge generated by both sectors can be subordinated to love. If that is done, then the dialogue between psychology and Christianity ought to be more amicable and fruitful. To the nonbeliever, I hope that this book has presented the insights of Jesus on human psychology in such a way that they can be viewed more sympathetically for at least the human wisdom they contain.

Having worked in a psychiatric hospital in St. Louis, Dennis Linn remarked that given all the hurts suffered by the people he met, there would be three choices open to them: to wind up in a psychiatric hospital, in a prison, or to grow more deeply in spiritual development.[36] That is something to ponder deeply when considering how psychology can be augmented by spiritual insights.

Notes

1. Needleman, J., *Lost Christianity* (Garden City: Doubleday, 1980), p. 156.

2. Gabbard, G. and Twemlow, S., "Explanatory Hypotheses for Near Death Experiences," paper presented at the convention of the American Psychological Association, Los Angeles, August, 1981, pp. 2–3.

3. Moody, R., *Life After Life* (New York: Bantam, 1975), pp. 182–183.

4. Ring, K., *Life at Death* (New York: Coward, McGann & Geoghegan, 1980), pp. 15–16.

5. Rawlings, in personal communication to Ring, cited by Ring, op. cit., pp. 248–249.

6. Moody, op. cit., p. 59.

7. Rawlings, M., interview with Pat Robertson, *700 Club*, 1981.

8. Ibid.

9. Talbot, M., *Mysticism and the New Physics* (New York: Bantam, 1980), pp. 144–145.

10. Maloney, G., *TM and Christian Meditation* (Pecos, NM: Dove, 1976). This apparent ability of entities from the nonphysical world to break into the physical world and take on a great variety of forms may help to explain some of the important differences in the near-death experiences of Christians as compared with those of Hindus.

11. Rath, R., "Silva Mind Control—Is it Really Demonic?" *Journal of Christian Healing*, vol. 2, no. 2, 1980, p. 4.

12. Green, E., and Green, A., *Beyond Biofeedback* (New York: Delta, 1977), pp. 320–321.

13. Ibid., p. 290.

14. Jung, C.G., *Memories, Dreams and Reflections* (New York: Random House, 1961), p. 276.

15. Hick, J., *Death and Eternal Life* (New York: Harper & Row, 1976). p. 67.

16. Ibid., p. 115.

17. All scriptural quotes are taken from *The Good News Bible* (New York: American Bible Society, 1976), unless otherwise indicated.

18. Hick, op. cit., p. 189.

19. Ring, op. cit., pp. 224–232.

20. Rivera, G., "The Shroud of Turin," report on *20/20*, ABC–TV, April 16, 1981; Wilson, I., *The Shroud of Turin* (Garden City: Doubleday, 1979).

21. Rawlings, p. 77.

22. Currie, I., *You Cannot Die* (New York: Meuthen, 1978), 193–194.

23. Needleman, *A Sense of the Cosmos*, p. 46.

24. Ibid., p. 129.

25. Kelsey, M., personal communication, 1973.

26. Freud, S., *Civilization and its Discontents* (New York: Norton, 1961), pp. 56–57.

27. Freud, S., cited by Kung, H., *Freud and the Problem of God* (New Haven: Yale, 1979), p. 121.

28. Ibid., p. 121.

29. Huvelin, Abbé, *Je n'aimerai jamais assez* (Paris: Fleurus, 1963).

30. Zimbardo, P., "The Age of Indifference," *Psychology Today*, August 1980, vol. 14, no. 3, pp. 74–76.

31. Frankl, V., *Man's Search for Meaning* (New York: Washington Square Press, 1962).

32. Kelsey, M., *Healing and Christianity* (New York: Harper & Row, 1976).

33. Jung, op. cit., p. 254.

34. Kelsey, M., *Afterlife: the Other Side of Dying* (New York: Paulist Press, 1979); Kelsey, M., *Healing and Christianity* (New York: Harper & Row, 1976); Kelsey, M., *The Art of Christian Love* (Pecos, NM: Dove, 1974); Linn, D. & Linn, M., *Healing Life's Hurts* (New York: Paulist Press, 1978); Linn, D. & Linn, M., *Healing of Memories* (New York: Paulist Press, 1974); Parkhurst, G., *Positive Living through Inner Healing* (Plainfield, NJ: Logos, 1973); Scanlan, M., *Inner Healing* (New York: Paulist Press, 1974).

35. Kelsey, *Healing and Christianity*, p. 57.

36. Linn & Linn, *Healing Life's Hurts*, pp. 5–6.

Bibliography

Barlow, D. H.; Abel, G. G.; and Blanchard, E. B. "Gender Identity Change in a Transsexual: An Exorcism." *Archives of Sexual Behavior,* vol. 6, no. 5, 1977.

Barrett, W. *The Illusion of Technique.* Garden City: Doubleday, 1978.

Bayless, R. *The Other Side of Death.* New Hyde Park, N.Y.: University Books, 1971.

Bergin, A. "Psychotherapy and Religious Values." Paper read at the Institute for the Study of Human Knowledge, New York, April, 1979. Published in *Journal of Consulting and Clinical Psychology,* 48, 1980.

Bergin, A., and Strupp, H., *New Frontiers in the Science of Psychotherapy.* New York: Aldine, 1972.

Binswanger, L. *Being-in-the-World.* New York: Basic Books, 1968.

Binswanger, L. "The Case of Ellen West: An Anthropological-Clinical Study," in *Existence.* Edited by Rollo May. New York: Simon & Schuster, 1958.

Campbell, D. "On the Conflicts between Biological and Social Evolution and between Psychology and Moral Tradition." Paper read at the American Psychological Association convention, Chicago, August, 1975. Reprinted in *American Psychologist,* December, 1975, pp. 1103–1126.

Currie, I. *You Cannot Die.* New York: Methuen, 1978.

Delooz, P. "Who Believes in the Hereafter?" In *Death and Presence,* Brussels: *Lumen Vitae,* 1970.

Fiore, C., and Landsburg, A. *Death Encounters.* New York: Bantam, 1979.

Frankl, V. *Man's Search for Meaning.* New York: Washington Square Press, 1962.

Freud, S. Letter to Albert Einstein (1934), cited in H. Kung, *Freud and the Problem of God.* New Haven: Yale, 1979.

Freud, S. *Civilization and Its Discontents.* New York: Norton, 1961.

Fromm, E. *The Crisis of Psychoanalysis.* Greenwich, Ct.: Fawcett, 1970.

Gabbard, G., and Twemlow, S. "Explanatory Hypotheses for Near Death Experiences." Paper read at the convention of the American Psychological Association, Los Angeles, August, 1981.

Gauld, A. "Discarnate Survival." In *Handbook of Parapsychology.* Edited by B. Wolman. New York: Van Nostrand Reinhold, 1977, pp. 577–630.

Green, E., and Green, A. *Beyond Biofeedback.* New York: Delta, 1977.

Greenhouse, H. B. *The Astral Journey.* New York: Avon, 1974.

Greenspoon, J. "The Reinforcing Effect of Two Spoken Sounds on the Frequency of Two Responses." *American Journal of Psychology,* 1955, 68, 409–416.

Grof, S., and Grof, C. *Beyond Death.* New York: Thames & Hudson, 1980.

Grof, S. Presentation made at conference on "Consciousness and Healing," Toronto, 1976. Cited in I. Currie. *You Cannot Die.* New York: Methuen, 1978.

Gross, M., *The Psychological Society,* New York: Random House, 1978.

Heidegger, M. *Being and Time.* Translated by J. Macquarrie and E. Robinson. New York: Harper & Row, 1962.

Hick, J. *Death and Eternal Life.* New York: Harper & Row, 1976.

Husserl, E. "The Crisis of European Sciences and Psychology." Paper read at Prague, 1935. Translated by D. Carr. In *Transcendental Phenomenology,* Chicago: Northwestern University Press, 1970.

Huvelin, A. *Je n'aimerai jamais assez.* Edited by M. Louis-Lefebvre. Paris: Fleurus, 1963.

Hyslop, J. H. *Psychical Research and the Resurrection.* Boston: Small and Maynard, 1908.

James, W. *The Will to Believe.* New York: Longmans-Green, 1937.

Jung, C. G. *Analytic Psychology: Its Theory and Practice.* New York: Random House, 1968.

Jung, C. G. *Memories, Dreams and Reflections.* New York: Knopf and Random House, 1961.

Kaplan, L. "A Theory of Mourning." Review of *Loss: Sadness and*

Depression, by John Bowlby. *New York Times Book Review,* August 24, 1980.

Kelsey, M. *Discernment.* New York: Paulist Press, 1978.

Kelsey, M. *Healing and Christianity.* New York: Harper & Row, 1976.

Kelsey, M. *The Other Side of Silence.* New York: Paulist, 1976.

Klein, H. A. *Holography.* New York: Lippincott, 1970.

Kristol, I. "Thoughts on Reading about a Number of Summer Camp Cabins Covered with Garbage." *New York Times Magazine,* November 17, 1964, p. 38.

Kübler-Ross, E. Interview on *Tomorrow Show,* February 14, 1978.

Küng, H. *Freud and the Problem of God.* New Haven: Yale, 1979.

Lasch, C. *The Culture of Narcissism.* New York: Norton, 1978.

Lilly, J. *The Center of the Cyclone.* New York: Julian, 1972.

Linn, M. and Linn, D. *Healing Life's Hurts.* New York: Paulist, 1978.

Linn, M. and Linn, D. *Healing of Memories.* New York: Paulist, 1974.

London, P. *The Modes and Morals of Psychotherapy.* New York: Holt, Rinehart and Winston, 1964.

Lowe, C. *Value Orientation in Counseling and Psychotherapy.* San Francisco: Chandler, 1969.

Lundahl, C. "The Near-death Experiences of Mormons." Paper read at the American Psychological Association convention, New York, 1979.

McDonagh, J. "Bibliotherapy with Suicidal Patients." Paper read at the American Psychological Association convention, New York, 1979.

Maloney, G. *TM and Christian Meditation,* Pecos, N.M.: Dove, 1976.

Maslow, A. *Towards a Psychology of Being.* New York: Van Nostrand, 1962.

Mattoon, M. *Applied Dream Analysis.* Washington: Winston, 1978.

May, R. *Love and Will.* New York: Norton, 1969.

May, R., ed. *Existence: A New Dimension in Psychiatry and Psychology.* New York: Simon and Schuster, 1958.

Monroe, R. A. *Journeys Out of the Body.* New York: Doubleday, 1971.

Moody, R. *Reflections on "Life After Life."* New York: Bantam, 1977.

Moody, R. *Life After Life.* New York: Bantam, 1975.

Needleman, J. *Lost Christianity.* Garden City: Doubleday, 1980.

Needleman, J. *On the Way to Self-Knowledge.* Edited by J. Needleman and D. Lewis. New York: Knopf, 1976.

Needleman, J. *A Sense of the Cosmos: The Encounter of Modern Science and Ancient Truth.* Garden City: Doubleday, 1975.

Needleman, J. *The New Religions.* Garden City: Doubleday, 1970.

Noyes, R., and Kletti, R. "The Experience of Dying from Falls." *Omega* 3:45–52.

Oden, T. "The New Pietism." *Journal of Humanistic Psychology* 12:24–41.

Office of Technology Assessment. *The Efficacy and Cost Effectiveness of Psychotherapy.* Washington, D.C.: U.S. House of Representatives, October, 1980.

Osis, K., and Haraldsson, E., *At the Hour of Death.* New York: Avon, 1977.

Ostrander, S., and Schroeder, S. *Psychic Discoveries Behind the Iron Curtain.* Englewood Cliffs, N.J.: Prentice-Hall, 1970.

Parkhurst, G. *Positive Living through Inner Healing.* Plainfield, N.J.: Logos International, 1973.

Parloff, M., et al. "Assessment of Psychosocial Treatment of Mental Health Disorders: Current Status and Prospects." Report to the National Academy of Sciences, Institute of Medicine, Washington, D.C., 1978.

Pattison, E. M. "Exorcism and Psychotherapy: A Case of Collaboration." In *Religious Systems and Psychotherapy.* Edited by R. H. Cox. Springfield, Ill: C. Thomas, 1973.

Pribram, K. "Holographic Memory." Interview in *Psychology Today* 12:70–84.

Progoff, I. *The Death and Rebirth of Psychology.* New York: Julian, 1956.

Quinn, S. "Oedipus vs. Narcissus." *New York Times Magazine,* November 9, 1980, p. 120.

Rath, R. "Silva Mind Control—Is It Really Demonic?" *Journal of Christian Healing,* 2:4.

Rawlings, M. Interview on the "700 Club" with Pat Robertson, 1981.

Rawlings, M. *Beyond Death's Door.* Nashville: Nelson, 1978.

Ricoeur, P. *De l'Interpretation: essai sur Freud.* Paris: Le Seuil, 1965.

Ring, K. *Life at Death.* New York: Coward, McCann & Geoghegan, 1980.

Rivera, G. "The Shroud of Turin." Report on "20/20," ABC-TV, April 16, 1981.

Rogo, D. S. *Parapsychology: A Century of Inquiry.* New York: Dell, 1975.

Sadler, W. *Existence and Love.* New York: Scribner, 1969.

Scanlan, M. *Inner Healing,* New York: Paulist, 1974.

Seiger, H. "Treatment of Essential Nocturnal Enuresis." *Journal of Pediatrics* 4:738–749.

Siegel, R. K. "The Psychology of Life after Death." *American Psychologist* 35:911–931.

Smith, M. L. *The Benefits of Psychotherapy.* Baltimore: Johns Hopkins University Press, 1980.

Spock, B. *Baby and Child Care.* New York: Simon and Schuster, 1976.

Szasz, T. *The Myth of Psychotherapy.* Garden City: Doubleday, 1978.

Talbot, M. *Mysticism and the New Physics.* New York: Bantam, 1980.

Tart, C. "Out-of-the-Body Experiences." In *Psychic Exploration.* Edited by Edgar Mitchell. New York: Putnam, 1974, pp. 349–373.

Tart, C. "A Psychophysiological Study of Out-of-the-body Experiences in a Selected Subject." *Journal of the American Society for Psychical Research* 62:21.

Tart, C. "A Second Psychophysiological Study of Out-of-the-body Experiences in a Gifted Subject." *Parapsychology,* vol. 9, December, 1967.

Vitz, P. *Psychology as Religion; The Cult of Self-Worship.* Grand Rapids, Mi.: Erdmans, 1977.

Watts, A. *Psychotherapy East and West.* New York: Pantheon, 1961.

Wilson, I. *The Shroud of Turin.* Garden City: Doubleday, 1979.

Zimbardo, P. "The Age of Indifference." *Psychology Today* 14:71–76.